The Business Environment

Tutorial

Alison Aplin

Published by Osborne Books Limited
Tel 01905 748071
Email books@osbornebooks.co.uk
Website www.osbornebooks.co.uk

Design by Laura Ingham

Printed by CPI Group (UK) Limited, Croydon, CR0 4YY, on environmentally friendly, acid-free paper from managed forests.

British Library Cataloguing in Publication Data
A catalogue record for this book is available from the British Library

ISBN 978-1-911198-56-7

Contents

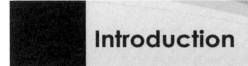

Introduction

Qualifications covered

This book has been written specifically to cover the Unit 'The Business Environment' which is mandatory for the following qualifications:

AAT Level 2 Certificate in Accounting

AAT Certificate in Accounting – SCQF Level 6

The book contains a clear text with worked examples and case studies, chapter summaries and key terms to help with revision. Each chapter concludes with a wide range of activities, many in the style of AAT computer based assessments.

Osborne Study and Revision Materials

Additional materials, tailored to the needs of students studying this Unit and revising for the assessment, include:

- **Workbooks:** paperback books with practice activities and exams
- **Wise Guides:** pocket-sized spiral bound revision cards
- **Student Zone:** access to Osborne Books online resources
- **Osborne Books App:** Osborne Books ebooks for mobiles and tablets

Visit www.osbornebooks.co.uk for details of study and revision resources and access to online material.

1 An introduction to business

this chapter covers...

This chapter gives an overview of different organisations which are in operation, identifying their main purpose as being profit making or not-for-profit.

The three main forms of business and their legal structure are described as:

- *sole traders*
- *partnerships*
- *companies*

Some business terms are introduced, such as the entity concept, incorporation and limited liability.

The key features of each type of business are explained and the aspects of control, management, liability, profit distribution and raising of finance are considered.

A summary of the content of financial statements for the three types of business and the areas of taxation that are relevant are explained.

All organisations have a variety of different functions, which are introduced in this chapter.

INTRODUCTION TO BUSINESSES

Before looking at what a business is, it is worth first of all considering, what is an organisation.

organisations

There are many different types of organisations that we come across in our daily lives, such as:

- schools
- hospitals
- shops
- charities
- sports clubs

Very simply, each organisation consists of a group of people working together to fulfil a purpose. For the examples above:

- schools provide education to children
- hospitals provide healthcare needs to individuals
- shops offer a variety of goods for sale, such as food, clothing, household, and personal items
- charities provide support for the social well-being of individuals
- sports clubs allow a group of people to participate in sporting activities

Each organisation will have its own set of motives (goals) which they are aiming to achieve, which could include:

- to provide a specific service
- to make money (a profit)
- to minimise pollution
- to provide employment
- to support a specific cause

Organisations may be profit making or not-for-profit organisations. In the examples we have looked at, shops will be profit making and the other organisations not-for-profit.

what is a business?

A business comprises one or more individuals selling goods and services to customers, with the primary motive to maximise profit.

Businesses differ greatly in terms of size, success and the range of goods and services offered for sale.

They may be:

- large supermarkets
- hairdressers
- technology businesses
- tradespeople, such as plumbers and electricians
- accountants

and many more.

profit

Profit is the difference between how much goods and services are sold for (revenue) and the business costs incurred. It is calculated as follows:

profit = total revenue – total costs

loss

If total costs exceed total revenue, a business will make a loss.

profit example

Kevin runs a business repairing motor vehicles. His sales revenue for last month was £16,500 and he incurred business costs of £11,000. Therefore Kevin's profit for the month was £5,500.

the entity concept

As you progress with your studies in accountancy you will learn many rules and regulations, one of them being accounting concepts. These are the principles which state how to record and report financial information for different organisations.

The entity concept means that the financial statements record and report on the activities (only) of one entity. They do not include the personal affairs of the owner/owners.

example of the entity concept

The financial statements of Jay Ltd only include the business transactions relating to the company; anything relating to the shareholders (owners) (for example their personal homes and/or mortgages) are not included.

TYPES OF ORGANISATIONS

Each type of business has a different legal structure, and this structure will determine the ability to grow the business and the financial impact on the business owners if things go wrong.

business types

There are three main types of business - sole traders, partnerships and companies. Each has a different legal structure.

- a **sole trader** is an individual who owns and runs a business; the individual makes all the decisions and has unlimited liability for the debts of the business. The amounts invested by the owner in the business are called capital.

sole trader example

Kevin who has a business repairing motor vehicles, started the business with £1,000 in capital from his savings.

He makes all of the decisions, such as how to advertise, who to sell to and the opening hours of the business.

If the business has debts that cannot be paid, such as rent or payments to suppliers, Kevin is personally responsible and must pay for them from his own money.

- a **partnership** is owned and run by one or more individuals. All partners are liable for the entire debts of the partnership; any decisions made are in accordance with the partnership agreement (written or verbal). The amounts invested by each partner are called capital.

partnership example

Carrie and Donovan run a café. They have arranged to share profits equally and each invested £5,000 of their own money into the business.

Donovan prepares all the food and Carrie is responsible for serving the customers. They agree the opening hours of the business and the content of the menu.

If the business has debts that cannot be paid, both Carrie and Donovan have unlimited liability. This means they are both personally responsible and must pay the debts from their own money. Therefore it is important that the partners trust each other.

- **companies** are referred to as **incorporated** businesses, meaning they are a separate legal entity from their owners, which allows the owners to have limited liability

  - a **private limited company (Ltd)** is owned by shareholders and run by directors on behalf of the shareholders. In many small companies these are often the same people. The liability of the shareholders is limited to the amount they originally invested (the share capital).

> **private limited company (Ltd) example**
>
> Micha has a business repairing motor vehicles called Micha Motor Repairs Ltd.
>
> Micha owns and runs the business and is therefore responsible for all the decisions made.
>
> Micha invested £100 of share capital in the business; therefore, his personal liability for the debts of the business is limited to this amount.

– a **public limited company (plc)** is owned by a minimum of two shareholders and often run by others (the directors, with a minimum requirement of two). The company must have share capital in excess of £50,000 and the shares can be available for members of the general public to buy through the stock market if the company chooses.

There are many examples of public limited companies, such as:

– Tesco plc

– Marks and Spencer Group plc

– John Lewis Partnership plc, which does not offer shares for sale to the general public

not-for-profit organisations

Some not-for-profit organisations are in the public sector, such as schools and hospitals. They are governed by the rules of national and local government. Public sector organisations are covered in more detail in the Level 3 Business Awareness unit.

Private sector not-for-profit organisations, such as local sports clubs and charities, use available resources acquired from fund raising, donations and subscriptions to provide support for their causes and activities. Charities are governed by a board of trustees and sports clubs are usually governed by an elected committee.

Charities must follow the rules of the Charities Act 2011 and are regulated by the Charity Commission. Their purpose must be for the public benefit.

Each charity will have a governing document which contains the aims of the charity and the rules for how it must operate. The trustees must abide by this document; failure to do so could mean having to repay the charity from their own money.

There are many examples of charities, such as:

■ The British Red Cross Society

■ Macmillan Cancer Support

■ BBC Children in Need

The website for the Charity Commission for England and Wales is:

www.gov.uk/government/organisations/charity-commission.

KEY FEATURES OF DIFFERENT BUSINESS TYPES

Each legal structure has advantages and disadvantages and we will consider each of these structures in terms of control, management, liability, profit distribution and the sources of finance available.

sole trader

A **sole trader** (also referred to as self-employed) owns the entire business and therefore has ultimate **control** and **management** of all business affairs.

Sole traders take **profits** out of the business in the form of drawings. Any profits not drawn from the business will increase the owner's capital, which is the amount that the business owes to the owner.

The **sources of finance** available to a sole trader include further capital from the owner, loans from other individuals and banks, bank overdraft facilities, credit from suppliers and leasing arrangements (which is similar to renting).

Advantages of a sole trader:

- a sole trader has no one to report to, they are their own boss
- all profits of the business belong to the owner
- there are no formal rules to follow
- the financial statements of a sole trader are private and not available to the public
- setting up a sole trader business is a straightforward process

Disadvantages of a sole trader:

- a sole trader is responsible for all aspects of the business, such as technology, marketing, and credit control
- there is no one to share ideas with
- a sole trader will often work long hours and it is difficult to have time off
- they have **unlimited liability** for the debts of the business and have the responsibility of any losses made by the business
- sole traders have limited growth capacity, due to the fact that they are owned by one individual
- sources of finance may be limited and guarantees (for example, an agreement by another person to repay a debt if the borrower defaults) may need to be made by the owner

partnerships

The **control** of a partnership is determined by the number of individuals involved and the agreement that has been reached between them. Each partner will have an active role in the business. A partnership agreement may state how the business is to be **managed** and responsibilities may be split or shared between partners, such as marketing, finance, operations and human resources.

Partnerships must follow the rules of the Partnership Act 1890 and any partnership agreement (written or verbal) which has been drawn up by the partners. A partnership agreement will include details on how profits and losses are divided between partners and their rights and responsibilities. If no agreement exists then profits and losses must be shared equally between all partners in accordance with the Act.

Partnership **profits** are distributed to partners in the same way as sole traders, through drawings.

The **sources of finance** available to partnerships are the same as those available to sole traders.

Advantages of a partnership:

- shared responsibilities mean that it is easier for individual partners to have time off and manage their working hours

- individual partners may be able to concentrate on their area of specialism. For example, partners in an accountancy business may specialise in business tax, personal tax, payroll, financial accounting, or management accounting

- partnerships have more potential to grow than sole traders, by increasing the number of partners

- the ability to raise further finance should be easier than for a sole trader, with the possibilities of introducing further capital from new partners, and it is generally easier for larger businesses to raise additional funds from external sources

- the only formal rules relate to the Partnership Act 1890 and any partnership agreement

- the financial statements of a partnership are private and there is no requirement to disclose them to the public

- setting up a partnership is a fairly straightforward process

Disadvantages of a partnership:

- individual partners will usually have no overall control of the business

- all profits of the business must be distributed between the partners

- all partners are liable for all **liabilities** of the partnership

- there may be disputes within the partnership which may be difficult to reconcile

There are other structures available for partnerships - Limited Liability Partnerships (LLPs) and Limited Partnerships.

limited liability partnership

A limited liability partnership (LLP) is an incorporated business with the members having limited liability.

There must be a minimum of two members, who can be individuals or companies (referred to as corporate members).

Unlike a partnership, the members are not personally liable for any debts that the business cannot pay.

An LLP agreement sets out how the business will be run, including:

- how profits are distributed between members

- members responsibilities

- the management and control of the LLP

- how members can join and leave the LLP

Sources of finance for an LLP are the same as those available to limited companies.

companies

Companies are **controlled** by shareholders and **managed** by directors.

Companies must follow the rules and regulations of the Companies Act 2006 and directors must submit annual financial statements and confirmation statements to Companies House (see Chapter 3 for further details).

Profits are distributed in the form of dividends. Dividends are the after tax distributions of a company which has reported a profit. They are agreed by the company directors and paid to shareholders.

A company may wish to raise additional funds along with the money provided by shareholders. In addition to the **sources of finance** available to sole traders and partnerships, further options are available:

- loans will traditionally come from banks and other financial institutions; however, smaller companies may raise additional finance from directors' loans

- debentures are long term unsecured loans which are taken out by companies and repaid at a specified date in the future and usually carry a fixed rate of interest

The advantages and disadvantages of a company will very much depend on the size of the business.

A **small one person limited company** has some similar advantages and disadvantages to those of a sole trader:

- **advantages**
  - own boss; no sharing of profits
- **disadvantages**
  - responsible for all areas; long hours

Whereas **larger companies** will have some similarities to partnerships:

- **advantages**
  - shared responsibility; specialisms
- **disadvantages**
  - shared profits; disputes

However, there are **further advantages** of operating as a company:

- a company is a separate legal entity; in a dispute it would be the company that would be sued, not the individual shareholders
- the shareholders have **limited liability**; they can only lose the amount they have invested
- companies have continuity; they will keep going even if there is a change in ownership
- there are potentially more sources of finance available
- some small businesses will register as a limited company in order to create a better impression in the business world

And **further disadvantages** of operating as a company include the following:

- formal processes must be followed to set up and administer a company, which results in higher administrative costs
- financial statements must be prepared in accordance with the Companies Act 2006 and Financial Reporting Standards (FRSs) or International Financial Reporting Standards (IFRSs)
- the financial statements are available for the general public to view as they are filed with Companies House, although the details available for smaller companies are minimal

THE CONTENT OF FINANCIAL STATEMENTS

As you progress with your studies you will become familiar with financial statements produced by businesses.

Unincorporated businesses (sole traders and partnerships) will usually prepare a statement of profit or loss and a statement of financial position; however, there is no legal requirement to do so and no set format.

- the **statement of profit or loss** – shows how a business has performed financially during a period, which is calculated as:

  income minus expenses = profit (or loss)

- the **statement of financial position** – shows what a business owns and how it is financed at the end of a financial period, which is calculated as:

  assets minus liabilities = capital

Incorporated businesses (all limited companies) must file statutory annual accounts with Companies House and make available their financial statements to shareholders.

The financial statements must be prepared in a specific format and follow the rules of the Companies Act 2006 and relevant Financial Reporting Standards (FRSs and IFRSs).

The financial statements include a **statement of profit or loss** and a **statement of financial position.**

limited company statement of profit or loss example

H Ltd

Statement of profit or loss for the year ended 31 March 20-1

	£000	£000
Revenue		3,803
Cost of sales		2,434
Gross profit		1,369
Less Expenses:		
Administration expenses	485	
Distribution expenses	79	
		564
Operating profit		805
Less Finance costs		27
Profit for the year before tax		778
Less Tax		162
Profit for the year after tax		616

limited company statement of financial position example

H Ltd

Statement of Financial Position as at 31 March 20-1

	£000 Cost	£000 Depreciation	£000 Carrying amount
Non-current Assets			
Plant and equipment	2,160	757	1,403
Current Assets			
Inventory		79	
Trade and other receivables		610	
Cash and cash equivalents		207	
		896	
Less Current Liabilities			
Trade and other payables	215		
Tax liabilities	162		
		377	
Net Current Assets			519
			1,922
Less Non-current Liabilities			465
NET ASSETS			1,457
EQUITY			
Ordinary shares			400
Share premium			100
Retained earnings			957
TOTAL EQUITY			1,457

At this stage in your studies you will not be expected to be able to produce financial statements.

In addition to the **statement of profit or loss** and **statement of financial position**, the financial statements include:

■ **notes** to the financial statements – these provide further detail on areas provided in the two main statements, for example specific accounting policies

■ **statement of cash flows** – shows the money going into and out of a company during an accounting period. It is based on figures drawn from the statement of profit or loss and the statement of financial position. Its main purpose is to highlight how much cash the business has at the end of the year, where it has come from and whether it has increased or decreased

In basic terms it states:

cash at the beginning of the year plus increase in cash during the year (or minus decrease in cash during the year) = cash at the end of the year

It is often said that 'Cash is King' – and this is absolutely true in relation to a business where a shortage of cash can cause a business to fail.

- **statement of changes in equity** – shows the changes that have taken place during an accounting period of the amounts that are attributable to the shareholders

limited company statement of changes in equity example

H Ltd

Statement of Changes in Equity for the year ended 31 March 20-1

	Share capital £000	Share premium £000	Retained earnings £000	Total £000
Balances at start	400	100	577	1,077
Profit for the year			616	616
Dividends paid			(236)	(236)
Balances at end	400	100	957	1,457

- **directors report** – includes a review of the business activities during the accounting period and any future developments

- **auditors report** – an independent review of the financial statements, which is carried out by an organisation which is external to the company; most smaller companies are exempt

Some large companies publish their financial statements along with an annual report online. Examples can be found by visiting the following websites:

- https://about.sainsburys.co.uk/investors/results-reports-and-presentations/2021

- https://www.tescoplc.com/investors/reports-results-and-presentations/annual-report-2021/

limited liability partnerships (LLPs)

LLPs must file statutory accounts with Companies House which must be available to the members, including:

- a statement of profit or loss account

- a statement of financial position

- notes to the financial statements

- a strategic report (unless exempt) – this is a fair review of the business and its principal risks and uncertainties

TAXATION PAYABLE BY BUSINESSES

Individuals and businesses pay tax to Her Majesty's Revenue & Customs (HMRC) on their income and profits.

HMRC is the government department in the UK that controls and administers all aspects of UK tax law.

The type of taxes paid by individual businesses will be dependent on their legal structure and size.

income tax

Payable by **individuals** on their earnings and investment income.

- earnings include the taxable profits of sole traders and partnerships (including LLPs)
- earnings also include income from employment. If a business has employees, income tax is deducted through the Pay As You Earn (PAYE) system

national insurance

Payable by employed and self-employed **individuals**, and **businesses** who have employees.

- self-employed include sole traders and partnerships (including LLPs)
- national insurance contributions are deducted through the PAYE system for businesses that have employees.

corporation tax

Payable by **companies** on their income (taxable profits) and gains.

LLPs

LLPs are not taxed in the same way as companies. The taxable profits are distributed to members (in accordance with the LLP agreement) and individual members pay income tax and national insurance on their profit share.

Value Added Tax (VAT)

Payable by the final consumer on many goods and services. VAT is an indirect tax, which means that the seller collects it on behalf of HMRC.

In the UK, VAT-registered businesses must charge VAT on the taxable goods and services they supply to customers.

There are a vast range of taxable goods and services; examples include fuel, motor vehicles equipment and furnishings.

Businesses must register for VAT if their supply of taxable goods and services exceed a certain limit, regardless of their legal structure.

BUSINESSES FUNCTIONS

Organisations have a variety of functions which support their success and smooth running.

the role of business functions

An individual business will have many different functions or departments which are shown in the table below and the following pages.

Each business function has a different role to play and will contribute to the success of a business in several ways.

business functions and the size of the business

The number of staff that perform each business function will vary according to the size and type of business. For example, in a small accountancy practice one partner may have responsibilities for human resources, with another taking on information technology, alongside their usual work.

function	role in business	contribution to business
finance	responsible for: ■ financial accounting ■ management accounting ■ treasury management ■ internal audit (in larger businesses)	■ monitoring and reporting on financial success (or failure) ■ ensuring that there are sufficient funds available to support activities ■ producing financial plans and forecasts
operations	responsible for all the activities which are involved in the production of a product or service *for example, the transformation of raw materials into finished goods*	■ ensuring that production can be run as efficiently as possible ■ ensuring a fair price is paid for purchases

function	role in business	contribution to business
sales and marketing	responsible for the selling and promotion of products and services	■ ensuring customers are made aware of products and services ■ ensuring that the needs of customers are met ■ sourcing new customers and markets
human resources	responsible for the management of the workforce in terms of: ■ recruitment ■ training ■ performance appraisal ■ remuneration, holiday and sickness entitlements ■ termination	■ ensuring all employment rules and regulations are met ■ ensuring that staff are retained
information technology	responsible for the computer-based information systems, including: ■ the internet ■ emails ■ software applications ■ computer hardware ■ sourcing new relevant technologies	■ ensuring that all systems are working correctly ■ ensuring that the needs of staff are met

function	role in business	contribution to business
distribution and logistics	responsible for all the activities which are required to deliver a product or service to the final customer, including: ■ receiving, storing and handling raw materials ■ storing, distributing and delivering finished products and services	■ ensuring the movement of raw materials and finished goods is performed effectively and efficiently ■ ensuring that all goods within warehouses are easy to locate, not damaged and in date

The role of the finance function is covered in more detail in Chapter 4.

integrated information technology

Different business functions require different types of software to carry out their activities, such as:

■ finance – accounting, taxation and payroll software

■ operations – production software

■ human resources – personnel software

Often a business will use integrated software which allows the different functions to work together, saving duplication of data. Small businesses may purchase off the shelf integrated software, with larger businesses purchasing or designing bespoke software to ensure that all needs are met.

Chapter Summary

- Organisations exist in many different forms, sizes, and purposes.

- Businesses include sole traders, partnerships, and companies.

- Not-for-profit organisations include the public sector, clubs, and charities.

- Charities must follow the rules of the Charities Act 2011.

- Sole traders and partnerships have unlimited liability.

- All companies are incorporated; shareholders have limited liability.

- Companies must follow the rules and regulations of the Companies Act 2006 and reporting standards.

- The requirements and content of financial statements vary according to the type of business.

- Taxes payable depend on the type and size of a business.

- Business functions include finance, operations, sales and marketing, human resources, information technology, distribution and logistics.

Key Terms

sole trader	one individual in business
partnership	a group of individuals working together in business
company	separate legal entity, run by directors and owned by shareholders
charities	run by trustees, the purpose must be for the public benefit
shareholders	the owners of companies
directors	the people who manage companies
profit	sales revenue less business costs
capital	amounts invested in a business by sole traders and partnerships
share capital	amounts invested by the owners (shareholders) of a company
drawings	amounts taken from a business by sole traders and partnerships

dividends	profits distributed to shareholders of companies
entity concept	financial statements include the business activities of one entity
taxation	payable by businesses and individuals on income received and profits
statement of profit or loss	shows how a business has performed financially during a financial period
statement of financial position	shows how much a business is worth
statement of cash flows	shows the cash going into and out of a business
statement of changes in equity	shows the changes in the worth of a company that is attributable to shareholders
directors report	a review of business activities over a financial period
auditors report	independent review of financial statements
business functions	responsible for different areas of organisations

Activities

1.1 Identify whether each of the following are profit or not-for-profit organisations:

Organisation		Profit	Not-for-profit
(a)	Further education colleges		
(b)	Chain of pubs		
(c)	Children's hospice		
(d)	Online bookshop		

1.2 Giovanna has a business producing electrical components. The primary motive of her business will be:

(a)	to use electric vehicles in transportation	
(b)	to support a local animal charity	
(c)	to maximise profit	
(d)	to provide training opportunities	

1.3 Identify whether the following statement is True or False:

Statement	True	False
The entity concept means that all transactions (both business and private) of a sole trader are included in the financial statements.		

1.4 Rosie runs a florist business. She is the only director and shareholder. The type of business is:

(a)	a sole trader	
(b)	a partnership	
(c)	a private limited company	
(d)	a public limited company	

1.5 Public limited companies must have a minimum share capital of:

(a)	£100	
(b)	£5,000	
(c)	£10,000	
(d)	£50,000	

1.6 Identify how profits are distributed to owners in the following types of business:

Business		**Drawings**	**Dividends**
(a)	Company		
(b)	Partnership		
(c)	Sole trader		

1.7 Identify two advantages and two disadvantages of a business operating as a partnership.

1.8 Discuss how a sole trader can raise funds to purchase a new piece of machinery.

1.9 List the contents of the financial statements of a large public limited company.

1.10 Benny, Denny and Penny are in partnership. They have five employees and the business is registered for VAT. Select **all** of the taxes that the business may need to pay:

(a)	income tax	
(b)	corporation tax	
(c)	national insurance	
(d)	VAT	

1.11 Complete the table below by selecting the business function that relates to each business activity from the following list:

Finance   **Operations**   **Sales and Marketing**   **Human resources**

Information technology   **Distribution and logistics**

Business activity	Business function
Monitoring the training needs of employees	
Negotiating with suppliers the quantities of material required for production	
Dealing with the transport of products overseas	

2 The external business environment

this chapter covers...

This chapter considers the environment in which businesses operate. The main focus is to understand what an economy is and to explore the economic factors which have an impact on the way that businesses perform and the decisions they make, including:

- *employment*
- *consumer income*
- *inflation*
- *interest rates*
- *taxation*
- *exchange rates*

The role of governments in controlling the economy is summarised.

Implications of competition and international trading are considered, along with an introduction to the concepts of demand and supply.

THE ECONOMY

The economy is the sale or trade of goods and services that have a value. When referring to the economy it may be global, or relate to a specific area, for example the UK economy or a local economy, such as a city or town.

the global economy

Businesses operate in a global economy and how this affects them directly will depend on their location, size, the types of goods and services they sell and who their customers are.

The global economy is unlikely to have a huge impact on a small hair salon, whereas the local economy will.

Businesses that trade internationally by selling goods and services overseas **(exports)** or buying goods and services from overseas **(imports)** will be affected by changes in the global economy.

Some businesses perform all of their operations globally and have offices around the world, such as HSBC and Amazon.

economic environment

The economic environment relates to all factors that have an impact on the decisions made by consumers when buying goods and services.

A consumer may be an individual or an organisation.

The factors include:

- levels of **employment** – the number of adults employed by organisations in the workforce
- levels of **consumer income** – the amounts consumers receive from their work, pensions and investments
- **inflation** – the annual rate of increases in the prices of goods and services
- **interest rates** – the amounts received from savings and charged on borrowings
- rates of **taxation**
- **exchange rates** – the price of one currency expressed in terms of another currency

These factors are called **macro-economic factors** and are outside of the control of businesses. Each one will be considered throughout this chapter.

The state of the economy impacts on how businesses perform and the decisions they make. For example, higher taxes will reduce spending.

UNCERTAINTY AND RISK

The primary motive of a business is to maximise profit, which was identified in Chapter 1.

However, businesses are faced with uncertainty and risk, which can have an impact on future profitability.

Risk means that something negative may happen in the future. However, risk can be measured with some probability; there is a number of possible outcomes and each one can be measured. For example, when throwing a dice we can state that the probability of throwing a three is one in six, or 16.67%. Businesses can measure risk based on past experience and managing risk is important to allow them to survive and flourish.

risk example

An established business had sales averaging £100,000 in each of the past 12 months in 2019.

When predicting sales for the next year, the business has estimated, based on past performance that there is a 90% probability that sales will exceed £100,000 each month.

Uncertainty is uncontrollable, it happens due to events outside of the control of a business and the outcome is unknown.

uncertainty example

The business in the example above is a restaurant. When the UK was put into lockdown in March 2020, due to the pandemic, monthly sales were £nil.

the global market

Businesses operate in a global market and the challenges they face include:

- **political and economic uncertainties**; these are outside of the control of businesses

- **operational risk,** such as the threat of fraud and to security

- **financial risk,** for example changes in currencies and interest rates, or the cost of launching a new product

- **compliance risk,** for example doing something wrong and facing legal proceedings

- **risks** relating to **competition and reputation,** such as new businesses entering the market or receiving bad press

GOVERNMENT CONTROL OF THE ECONOMY

Governments will usually attempt to control the economy in four key areas:

- **growth**, which is the annual percentage increase in Gross Domestic Product (GDP)

  - GDP is the total value of all goods and services produced by an economy in one year

  - it is important to individual countries, as the standard of living is improved as GDP increases

- **inflation,** the rate at which the prices for goods and services rise

  - many countries seek low inflation and stable prices

overseas trading example

If a country, for example, the UK, has high inflation, there will be an impact on UK businesses that trade globally. The goods or services from UK businesses will be more expensive than ones that can be sourced from other countries. The consequence will be a fall in demand from overseas for the goods and services from UK businesses.

- **employment** – trying to ensure that individuals who want a job have one

- **balance of payments** – the value of imports into and exports out of a country should be broadly in balance

  - if **imports exceed exports**, the amount of money leaving a country will be higher than the money coming in and this will have to be financed; it is referred to as a **trade deficit**

  - if **exports exceed imports**, the amount of money coming into a country will be higher than the money going out. This will lead to higher inflation as the demand within the country increases; it is referred to as a **trade surplus**

raising finance

Governments raise finance through taxation. Local or central government set the amount of taxes that individuals and businesses must pay.

Taxes are classified as:

- **direct** – which are paid directly to the government

- **indirect** – which are collected by organisations on behalf of the government

an effective tax system

The key principles of a good tax system were formulated many years ago in 'The Wealth of the Nations (1776)' which stated they should follow the four principles of **fairness, certainty, convenience** and **efficiency**.

These principles are still used today and an effective tax system should cover the principles of:

- **equity** – individuals or businesses who have the same income levels are treated equally

- **certainty** – the rules should not change for transactions that have occurred in the past, allowing taxpayers to calculate the amount due and know when they should be paid

- **convenience** – the method of tax collection should be easily facilitated

- **economy** – the costs to taxpayers and the government for collecting taxes should be kept to a minimum and the system should be in line with the economic goals of the economy

- **fairness** – the amounts of tax paid by individuals and businesses with different levels of income should be fair

- **transparency** – the system should have clear rules which are understandable.

the UK tax system

In the UK, Her Majesty's Revenue & Customs (HMRC) collects taxes from various sources to make sure money is available to fund the UK's public services (for example, the National Health Service (NHS), defence, policing and education), to help families and individuals with targeted financial support (for example, the payment Universal Credit) and to fund the state pension.

The sources of UK taxes include:

- **direct taxes** – income tax, corporation tax, capital gains tax, inheritance tax, national insurance contributions, council tax (a charge on residential property) and business rates

- **indirect taxes** – Value Added Tax (VAT) and excise duties on products such as petrol, tobacco and alcohol

the economic cycle

Economies generally follow a pattern, known as the economic cycle. The cycle looks at the Gross Domestic Product (GDP) of an economy for a financial quarter and the pattern will generally include periods of:

- **boom,** which is an upturn in economy and the GDP is increasing

- economic **slowdown**

- **recession**, where the GDP is in decline for two successive quarters

- **recovery**

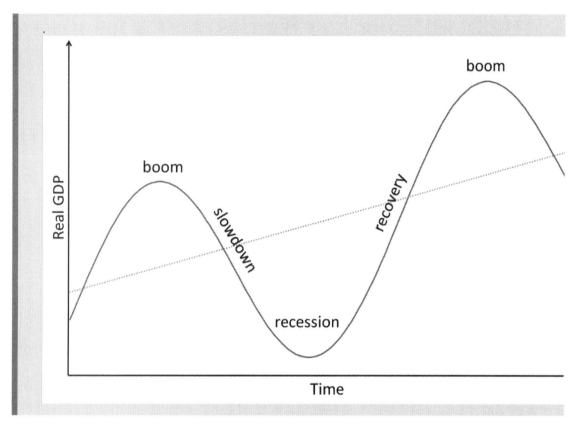

The current state of an economic cycle will affect decisions made by governments.

EMPLOYMENT

The levels of employment or unemployment in an economy will affect businesses in different ways.

An individual is classed as unemployed if they are actively seeking employment but cannot find a job.

Low unemployment is likely to lead to an increase in wage costs for businesses, as employees demand higher salaries.

The consequences of **high unemployment** for businesses are:

- **slow economic growth**, due to individuals who are available for work not being fully utilised

- **falls in consumer spending**, as a result of a drop in household income
    - this will mean a reduction in sales for many businesses
    - however, some businesses offering low cost alternatives may see an increase in sales

- businesses that are recruiting have **more choice** and may be able to offer **lower pay** (subject to minimum wage restrictions)

government and levels of employment

Governments usually seek to keep levels of employment as high as possible and levels of unemployment as low as possible.

High levels of unemployment can have detrimental effects on the economy:

- governments will need to support the unemployed by paying benefits

- unemployment is often linked to poor health and a rise in crime

- economic growth can be restricted as resources are being wasted

In the UK, the government offers incentives to businesses to encourage them to employ more staff; examples include:

- **apprenticeships**, where employees spend a minimum of 20% of their time completing off the job training, the employer must pay at least the Apprenticeship National Minimum Wage and the employer may receive a financial incentive

- **industry placements (T levels)**, a 45 day placement for 16 to 19 years olds, there is no cost to the employer and they may receive a financial incentive

- the **kickstart scheme**, a six month work placement for 16 to 24 year olds, the wages are subsidised by the government up to predetermined limits and the employer may receive additional funding to cover training and start-up costs

There are also incentives to retain existing staff, such as reducing the national insurance contributions payable by smaller organisations who meet certain conditions, known as the **Employment Allowance,** and in more recent times the **furlough scheme.**

the furlough scheme

When the world was hit by the coronavirus pandemic, many employees lost their jobs and others were put at risk, due to employers being forced to close or having big reductions in their sales.

The UK government introduced the Coronavirus Job Retention Scheme, also known as the furlough scheme, to allow affected eligible employers to claim from the government up to 80% of their employee's gross wages, subject to a maximum of £2,500 per employee per month.

CONSUMER SPENDING

Levels of consumer income affect the ways that consumers spend. This will impact businesses in different ways:

- **increases in consumer income** – consumers will be looking to increase spending and there will be an increase in demand for luxury items (for example holidays) and a decrease in demand for basic items (for example second-hand goods)

- **decrease in consumer income** – consumers will have less money to spend and there will be a fall in demand for luxury items, as they will seek to make do with what they already have. The demand for basic items (for example supermarket own brand items) will increase

government and consumer spending

Governments will want to see levels of consumer spending increase in order to boost an economy.

the eat out to help out scheme

The UK government introduced the Eat Out to Help Out Scheme in August 2020 in order to support the hospitality sector, which had been detrimentally affected by Covid-19, and to encourage consumer spending.

Consumers were able to spend money in participating businesses at a discounted rate, which was funded by the government.

Businesses that encounter a fall in the cost of their goods or services may choose to pass the reduction in cost onto their customers, or they may choose to increase profitability. The decisions a business makes will be determined by the current demand for goods and services.

INFLATION

Inflation is the general increase in the level of prices.

The rate of inflation is expressed as a percentage. Data is analysed using index numbers, which allow trends to be identified more easily.

The Retail Price Index (RPI) is used in the UK to measure inflation.

The Consumer Price Index (CPI) is used to measure how the prices of a typical basket of items change over time. The basket represents a set of goods and services purchased by a typical household and it changes from time to time to reflect changes in the habits of consumers.

High inflation means that consumers will spend less and the consequence for businesses is that their sales will fall.

Deflation is the opposite to inflation and is the reduction in the general level of prices. It occurs when the rate of inflation falls below 0% and can also be referred to as negative inflation. Deflation means that consumers will have more to spend, due to the decrease in the cost of goods and services.

EXCHANGE RATES

The exchange rate measures the quantity of foreign currency that can be bought with one unit of another.

For example, £1 buys €1.15 and £1 buys $1.39 USA dollars.

The rate of exchange is determined by the supply and demand on international currency markets.

costs to businesses

A strong currency makes imports cheaper but exports more expensive.

A weak currency makes imports more expensive but exports cheaper.

exchange rate example

Dy Ltd buys goods from France which cost €1,000. The exchange rate is £1 = €1.15.

The cost to Dy Ltd of importing the goods from France is £869.56 (€1,000 ÷ €1.15).

If the exchange rate changed to £1 = €1.25, meaning that the pound is stronger, the cost to Dy Ltd would decrease to £800.00 (€1,000 ÷ €1.25).

INTEREST RATES

Interest rates are expressed as a percentage. The rate will determine how much savers receive and how much borrowers are charged.

- **savers** receive interest on their savings, for example from bank deposit accounts
  - an increase in interest rates will encourage them to save more
  - a decrease in interest rates will encourage them to save less and savers may consider alternatives for any surplus funds, such as spending more

interest rate savings example

Hu Ltd has invested £100,000 in a bank deposit account. The interest rate is 2.5% per annum.

The interest which Hu Ltd would receive for the year is £2,500.

If the interest rate was 5%, Hu Ltd would receive £5,000 for the year, which may encourage Hu Ltd to save money. However, if the interest rate was 0.5%, Hu Ltd would only receive £500 for the year and may consider putting the £100,000 to better use, such as investing in equipment.

- **borrowers** are charged interest on amounts borrowed, for example from bank loans and mortgages
  - an increase in interest rates will discourage borrowers, as the interest charged will increase and the borrower will have to pay more money
  - a decrease in interest rates will encourage them to borrow more, as the amount they have to repay will fall
  - the rate of interest charged for borrowers is usually higher than the rate received by savers

government and interest rates

During a recession, governments will want interest rates to be as low as possible to encourage consumers to spend and borrow more, in order to boost the economy.

In the UK, the Bank of England sets the official interest rate, called the bank rate. This has a direct influence on the cost of savings, loans and mortgages for businesses and individuals.

MICRO-ECONOMIC ENVIRONMENT

The micro-economic environment relates to factors that have a direct impact on businesses and, unlike macro-economic factors, over which businesses have some control or influence.

Micro-economic factors include:

- the size of the available market for a product or service

- demand for a business's products or services

- competition

- the availability and quality of suppliers used by businesses to produce their goods and services

- the reliability of the distribution chain.

the forces of demand and supply

The **market price** is the amount that consumers are charged for goods and services; it is determined by:

- **demand** – the quantity that consumers are prepared to buy at different prices

  - demand will increase as prices fall

  - demand will decrease as prices rise

This can be illustrated graphically:

  - when the price (P) is high, the demand will contract and the quantity (Q) will be lower

  - a lower price (P) will cause an expansion in demand and the quantity (Q) will increase

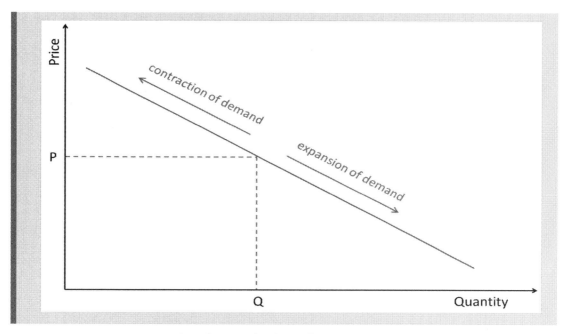

- **supply** – the quantity that sellers are prepared to offer for sale at different prices

    - supply (S) will increase as prices rise, as businesses can make more profit, as shown in the following graph

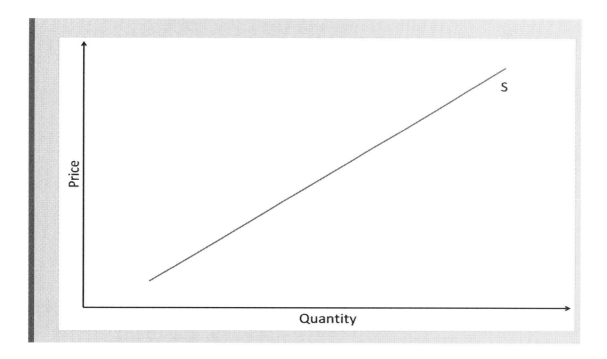

When the demand and supply patterns change, the market price will also change. For example:

- successful marketing campaigns will increase demand, which will usually cause a price increase

- competitors entering into an existing market can cause the price to decrease

competition

Competitiveness is the extent to which a business can stand up to or beat its rivals.

All businesses face competition, for example supermarkets. Plans of most businesses are affected by the behaviour and reactions of their competitors. A plan to increase the price of a particular product by Tesco for example would have to be revised, if a competitor, such as Asda, decided to reduce the price of the same product.

Examples of companies that compete in a global market include:

- fast food chains, such as McDonalds, KFC, Subway and Starbucks

- social media platforms, for example Facebook, Instagram, Twitter and LinkedIn.

Competition in a global market affects businesses by forcing them to compete internationally for both customers and staff.

international trading

A business which chooses to trade internationally will face risk and uncertainties and in addition **disadvantages**, including:

- language and cultural barriers

- operating according to different rules and regulations

- operating in different time zones

- the logistics involved in delivering goods

- payment issues and cash flow

However, there are also **advantages** to trading internationally, such as:

- there is a much larger market

- higher profit margins

- providing goods and services which are in scarce supply

Exchange rates could be an advantage or disadvantage, depending on whether a business is importing or exporting and the strength of the currency.

Chapter Summary

- The economy is the sale or trade of goods and services.

- The global economy is worldwide.

- The economic environment is all factors that influence consumers.

- Risk means that something bad may happen in the future, but can be measured with some probability. Uncertainty is uncontrollable.

- Governments attempt to control the economy in the areas of growth, inflation, employment and balance of payments.

- Governments raise finance through taxation.

- An effective taxation system should cover the principles of equity, certainty, convenience, economy, fairness and transparency.

- Demand is the quantity that consumers are prepared to buy.

- Supply is the quantity that sellers are prepared to offer for sale.

Key Terms		
	macro-economic factors	factors that are outside the control of organisations
	micro-economic factors	factors over which organisations have a degree of control
	consumer	an individual or organisation who purchases products or services
	employment	number of adults employed in the workforce
	consumer income	income from employment, pensions and investments
	inflation	the rate of increases in the prices of goods and services
	deflation	a reduction in the general level of prices
	interest rate	amounts received from savings and charged on borrowings
	exchange rate	one currency expressed in terms of another
	Gross Domestic Product (GDP)	total value of goods and services produced by an economy in one year
	growth	annual percentage increase in GDP
	economic cycle	the GDP of an economy for a quarter
	imports	buying from overseas
	exports	selling overseas
	balance of payments	balancing the value of imports and exports
	HM Revenue & Customs	the UK government department with responsibility for taxation
	direct taxation	taxation paid by individuals and organisations directly to the government
	indirect taxation	taxation collected on behalf of the government

Activities

2.1   The price of one currency in terms of another currency is called:

(a)	the tax rate	
(b)	inflation	
(c)	the exchange rate	
(d)	the interest rate	

2.2   Identify which **two** of these businesses are likely to sell more if consumer income rises:

(a)	jewellery shop	
(b)	second-hand clothing shop	
(c)	pound shop	
(d)	travel agent	

2.3   When there is inflation, prices will:

(a)	stay the same	
(b)	rise	
(c)	fall temporarily	
(d)	fall permanently	

2.4   An unemployed individual is defined as:

(a)	someone without a job who is in education	
(b)	someone without a job who is unable to work	
(c)	someone without a job who is actively seeking employment	

2.5   What would happen if the exchange rate of the Euro increases against the pound?

(a) EU goods would become cheaper to buy in the UK	
(b) UK businesses would expect to sell less in the EU	
(c) UK goods would become cheaper to buy in the EU	

EU = European Union

2.6   An increase in interest rates encourages increases in:

(a) savings	
(b) borrowing	
(c) consumer spending	

2.7   Identify whether following statements are true or false:

	True	False
A business which has offices in several countries must perform all financial operations in one country.		
A business which operates globally has an increased risk of its data being compromised.		

2.8   Complete the following sentence:

	Rise	Fall
As prices increase, demand will		
and supply will		

2.9   Explain the difference between risk and uncertainty.

2.10   List four ways a government attempts to control an economy.

2.11   Give three examples of a direct tax.

2.12   List the four stages of the economic cycle.

3 Rules and regulations for businesses

this chapter covers...

This chapter gives an overview of the principles of law in England and Wales, which operates a common law system combining legislation and case law.

The role of the UK Parliament and the courts system is summarised.

Different classifications of law are explained:

- *common law and equity*
- *criminal law and civil law*
- *public law and private law*

Contract law is introduced, and the elements that are essential to all contracts are discussed.

Different types of contract are explained and the consequences of a breach of contract.

The chapter also covers the rules and regulations that must be followed when a business is formed, the returns that must be submitted and the records that must be kept.

THE PRINCIPLES OF LAW

what is law?

Law is a set of principles and regulations which are set by government. They are used to govern the behaviour of society.

In the UK, English law relates to the legal system of England and Wales, with Scotland and Northern Ireland having separate legal systems.

England and Wales operate a common law system which combines the passing of legislation and creating precedents through case law.

the UK Parliament

The UK Parliament consists of the reigning monarch (the King), the House of Commons and the House of Lords.

The **House of Commons** is the democratically elected house of the UK Parliament, responsible for making laws and checking the work of government.

Membership to the **House of Lords** is either hereditary, or by appointment or official function. It plays a crucial role in examining bills, questioning government action and investigating public policy.

Legislation is passed through the UK Parliament. Once it has been approved, it is called an **Act of Parliament**.

An Act of Parliament is a law, enforced in all areas of the UK where it is applicable.

A **Bill** is a draft law; it becomes an Act of Parliament if it is approved by a majority in the House of Commons and House of Lords, and formally agreed to by the reigning monarch (known as **Royal Assent**).

the court system

The role of courts is to determine the outcome of legal disputes.

Case law is established through the courts system.

In England and Wales different cases are dealt with in the courts system, and depending on the type of court, the proceedings involve people such as:

- judges – a public officer who is appointed to decide cases in law courts
- magistrates – volunteers who hear court cases in their community
- jury – a group of individuals from the general public, who have been chosen to listen to the facts in a court case and to deliver a verdict of guilty or not guilty

The courts system consists of:

- County Court – for most civil cases, over which judges preside

- Tribunals – for matters such as employment and education; the proceedings are carried out by a judge along with panel members

- Family Court – for most family cases, over which judges and magistrates preside

- Magistrate's Court – for most criminal cases and some civil cases; the proceedings are performed by judges and magistrates

- Crown Court – for some criminal cases; the proceedings are undertaken by a judge along with a jury

- High Court – the third highest court, it deals with civil cases and appeals of decisions made in lower courts. Proceedings are undertaken by high court and deputy court judges

- Court of Appeal - the second highest court within the senior courts of England and Wales, it deals only with appeals from other courts or tribunals. There are two divisions, criminal and civil. The judges of the Court of Appeal are the Lord Chief Justice for criminal cases and the Master of the Rolls for civil cases, along with court of appeal judges

- UK Supreme Court – the highest court, which hears appeals on arguable points of law of the greatest public importance, for the whole of the United Kingdom in civil cases, and for England, Wales and Northern Ireland in criminal cases

how the law is classified

Laws can be classified in a number of different ways. The ones that we will consider are:

- common law and equity

- criminal law and civil law

- public law and private law

common law and equity

Common law has existed since the time of the Norman Conquest in 1066. It was developed from local customs and decisions that had been made in previous cases (known as precedent).

With common law a claimant who wins a case is rewarded a remedy in the form of damages.

Damages are not always a suitable remedy for all cases and therefore equity introduced fairness into the English legal system.

Equity allows the court to grant discretionary remedies, such as injunctions, specific performance, rectification, and rescission.

Different types of equitable remedy are explained below:

	types of remedy
damages	monetary compensation for loss or injury
injunction	restraining a person from beginning or continuing an action which threatens or invades the legal right of another
specific performance	requires that the work in a contract must be carried out
rectification	to correct an error or put something right
rescission	the withdrawal or cancellation of a contract

criminal law and civil law

Criminal law relates to crime, for example murder, manslaughter, theft, sexual offences, offences involving the misuse of drugs and terrorist offences.

The purpose of criminal law is to preserve social order by punishing wrongdoers and deterring others from committing crimes.

Civil law relates to a civil wrong. Examples include a breach of contract, negligence, slander, employment law disputes and cases involving the sale of goods.

The purpose of civil law is to compensate a person who has suffered a loss or injury due to the acts or omissions of others.

The differences between criminal and civil law cases are illustrated on the following page:

	criminal law	civil law
parties in the case	the state (R) (the King) prosecutes the defendant *NB. R refers to the reigning monarch*	the person who has suffered the loss (the claimant) initiates a claim against the defendant (the person alleged to have caused the loss or injury)
courts involved	first heard in either the Magistrates Court or the Crown Court	first heard in either the County Court or the High Court and sometimes the Magistrate's Court
burden of proof	the prosecution must prove the guilt of the defendant beyond reasonable doubt	the claimant must prove their case on a balance of probabilities
outcome of the case	if innocent the defendant is acquitted if guilty the defendant is convicted and sentenced	if the claimant wins the case, they are awarded a remedy if the claimant loses the case, they are not awarded a remedy

public law and private law

The aim of public and private law is to create social order.

Public law relates to the relationship between individuals and the government. It deals with matters relating to the country as a whole, such as:

■ criminal law
■ constitutional law – Acts of Parliament and case law
■ human rights law
■ administrative law – which governs the activities of the administrative agencies of the government, such as the police, international trade and taxation

Private law concerns laws that regulate the relationships between individuals, such as:

■ family law
■ contract law
■ company law

international sources

Since 1973, European Union (EU) law took precedence over domestic law to such an extent that Acts of Parliament that fail to comply with EU legislation can be superseded by the courts. This ended when the UK left the EU after Brexit.

EU legislation which applied directly or indirectly to the UK before 11.00 p.m. on 31 December 2020 (pre Brexit) has been retained in UK law as a form of domestic legislation known as 'retained EU legislation'.

THE PRINCIPLES OF CONTRACT LAW

what is a contract?

A contract is a legally binding agreement which is enforceable in a court of law.

Contracts are agreements between two parties. They may be in writing or are verbal. Examples of business contracts are:

- a written contract has been signed for the purchase of goods

- a verbal contract for goods which have been ordered over the telephone

In both examples one party to the contract does something in return for money.

A contract is **an agreement with legal consequences**. If the work done is not satisfactory, or if the payment is not made, the wronged party can take the other person to court for **breach of contract,** which is an example of a civil wrong.

Contract law affects many business arrangements.

For example:

- if a business quotes an incorrect price to a customer, the customer may be able to hold the business to that price, under the terms of the contract of sale

- if a business fails to finish a job for a customer, the customer may be able to go to court to obtain a court order for the business to complete the work under the contract

the elements of a contract

There are three elements which are common and essential to all contracts:

elements of a contract

1 - agreement – an offer and an acceptance

2 - consideration – some value is exchanged

3 - intention to create legal relations

The three elements of a contract will be explained in turn.

The parties to a contract must have the **capacity**, or ability, **to contract and submit** themselves to the authority of the law.

For example, persons under the age of eighteen (minors) and persons of unsound mind or under the influence of alcohol have limitations on their power to contract.

1 - agreement – an offer and an acceptance

the offer

An **offer** may be made by:

- the **seller** of goods and services to an individual, a group, or generally to anyone who wishes to make a purchase, or . . .

- the **buyer** of goods and services who wishes to place a definite order for goods or services

The acceptance of an offer – from the seller or the buyer – will then form the basis of a **legally binding contract** which can be upheld in a court of law.

invitation to treat

An offer is quite different from an **invitation to treat** which is an invitation to an individual or business to make an offer.

A business offering its goods for sale online is making an invitation to treat. A customer who sees the goods online, can proceed to issue a purchase order or place an order at the current price which will be agreed between the business and the customer.

invitation to treat example

Alice sees a stand up desk advertised online for £50. She telephones the supplier who tells her that the figure is an error – it should have been £500. Alice insists on buying the desk for £50. The problem is, does a contract exist on the basis of the £50 quoted?

solution

Alice has no rights here. There is no contract because the £50 quoted online is only **an invitation to treat**. The company will clearly not agree to £50 for the stand-up desk.

termination of an offer

An offer may only be accepted while it is still open for acceptance. An offer may be terminated in the following circumstances:

- the time limit (if there is one) expires; if there is no time limit, the offer lapses after a reasonable period of time

- the offeror – the person making the offer – may revoke (cancel) the offer

- an offer may be rejected by the making of a counter-offer

  for example, if you offer your car for sale for £11,500 and someone offers you £10,000, that is a counter-offer

- by acceptance or rejection of the offer

acceptance of an offer

Acceptance of an offer must be firm and unambiguous; it may be in spoken words, written form or even implied by action. Acceptance cannot be assumed from silence on the part of the person to whom the offer is made.

For example, if you say, "I offer you my car for £11,500; if I have not heard from you within a week I will assume the deal is done", there is no acceptance. The offeree may go on holiday, or forget it even happened.

Acceptance must also be **unconditional**. Any new term introduced – *"I will agree to buy your car as long as the radio is replaced"* – amounts to a counter-offer and will revoke the original offer.

The term **"subject to contract"**, often seen on estate agents' boards, means that the terms of the offer to the offeree seem satisfactory, but have not been finally accepted. The two parties involved have agreed to draw up a formal contract for signature at a later date. There is no binding contract at this point.

2 - consideration – some value is exchanged

A valid contract involves **consideration,** which is passing a value between the two parties in a contract. If a business buys goods, there is a two way process involved:

- the supplier promises to deliver the goods (the promisor)

- the buyer agrees to pay for them (the promisee)

The **consideration** is the value given by both parties:

- the payment – the price paid by the buyer for the goods provided

- the value of the goods handed over by the supplier

Consideration must by law be **sufficient.** This means that:

- it must have value (not necessarily money or goods), although the value need not be adequate in some eyes

    for example, you could sell this book for 5p; many might think the amount to be inadequate, but the 5p still has value and is therefore consideration

- it must be sufficient, ie it must be in return for the promise (which may be to do something in the future); money due for some other reason or obligation is not sufficient consideration

The person who is promised goods or a service **must themselves provide payment** if the promise is to be enforceable as a contract. If you buy goods, you must make the payment. If someone else pays for you (an unlikely event!), you cannot take the supplier to court if the goods do not arrive.

The consideration **should not happen before the promise**. If you mend someone's car without any mention of payment, and the car owner the following week promises to give you £50, and subsequently refuses to pay you, there is no contract. The promise of payment followed the service provided.

consideration example

Harry runs a computer maintenance business and promises to repair a computer for a friend free of charge one weekend. Unfortunately, Harry wipes all the data from the computer and it cannot be replaced. His friend says he will sue Harry. Can he? Is there a contract?

solution

No. There is no contract because there is no consideration – no money has been paid. Harry has made a mistake but he cannot be sued.

3 - intention to create legal relations

A contract is an agreement involving consideration which the parties intend to be legally binding. In other words the parties entering a contract can reasonably expect the agreement to be enforced in a court of law if the need arises. The law assumes:

- commercial agreements are intended to be legally binding

- social and domestic arrangements are **not** intended to be legally binding

In short, if a person enters a contract to buy your car and then, without reason, refuses to pay for it, you can take him or her to court. If you ask a friend out for the evening, promising to take him or her out for a meal, and your friend doesn't turn up, you cannot take court action. The sale of a car involves the intention to create legal relations, the invitation out does not.

Contract terms may be classified as follows:

express terms — explicitly stated terms which are binding on both parties to the contract

conditions — fundamental terms of the contract which, if broken, will enable the injured party to reject the contract and to go to court to sue for damages

warranties — minor terms which if broken can be cause for an action for damages for loss suffered; the contract, however, remains in force

implied terms — terms which are not stated, but which are implied by trade custom or by law; for instance, goods sold should be of "satisfactory quality", in accordance with the Consumer Rights Act

In short:

- express terms are written into the contract; implied terms are not

- conditions are important terms, warranties are less important

types of contracts

A **valid** contract is a legally binding agreement.

A **void** contract is one that **cannot be enforced by law**. An agreement to carry out an illegal act or an agreement that is impossible to carry out are examples of void contracts.

A **voidable** contract is a valid contract that **can be nullified** (to make legally null and void) – one party is bound to a contract but the other party is not, so can withdraw from the contract. A contract between an adult and a minor is an example of a voidable contract as the adult is bound by the contract but the minor is not as they are not of legal age (capacity).

discharge of a contract

There are a number of situations where a contract will come to an end and no longer be legally binding. These include:

- **performance**: this is where all that is required in a contract has been performed, for example a car is sold, handed over by the car dealer to the customer and paid for

- **impossibility of performance**: this is where the circumstances dictate that the contract takes place, for example if one of the parties dies in a traffic accident

- **by prior agreement**: where the parties involved in the contract agree in writing beforehand that if a certain event takes place then either of the parties can give notice and pull out of the contract

- **rescission**: means a termination of the contract because one of the parties made a mistake or misrepresented the facts

- **breach of contract**: one of the terms of a contract has been broken.

the consequences of a breach of contract

A contract normally contains certain terms which must be fulfilled as part of the agreement. If a person breaks one of those terms, that person is in **breach of contract**.

*For example, if a supplier undertakes to supply goods, it must send the goods on the due date, and in turn expects the goods to be paid for by a certain time. If the customer does not pay, he or she is in breach of contract and may be taken to court for **damages** (money compensation).*

*Legal action can be taken against a customer when a contract is in existence because non-payment is a **breach of contract.***

Earlier in the chapter we saw that there are a number of **remedies** available for claimants in the courts system and this includes remedies for breach of contract.

The actual remedy chosen will depend on the type of contract.

*For example, a builder who is contracted to build a house and disappears off site before putting the roof on, can be ordered by the court to complete the work – this is the remedy of **specific performance**.*

pre-incorporation contracts

In the next section we will look at how different types of businesses are formed.

In Chapter 1 we saw that when a limited company is set up as a business, it is referred to as **incorporated** and has a separate legal identity from the business owners.

A pre-incorporation contract means that an individual has entered into a contract before the company has been registered.

In this case the individual is liable under the terms of the contract:

- prior to the incorporation of the company – the company does not have contractual capacity
- after incorporation of the company – the company cannot adopt a pre-incorporation contract.

FORMING A BUSINESS

There are rules and regulations that must be followed when businesses are formed.

When an individual, or a group of individuals, decide that they want to set up a business, one of their first decisions is to decide on the structure. In Chapter 1 the three business types discussed were:

- sole trader – one individual in business
- partnership – a group of individuals working together in business
- company – a separate legal entity, which is run by directors and owned by shareholders

Once the structure of the business has been decided, the next step is to form the business.

SETTING UP A BUSINESS AS A SOLE TRADER

the business name

A sole trader can trade under their own name, or they can choose another name for the business. The name does not need to be registered anywhere.

The name of the sole trader and the business name must be shown on official paperwork, for example invoices and letters.

Sole trader names must not:

- include 'limited', 'Ltd', 'limited liability partnership', 'LLP', 'public limited company' or 'plc'
- be offensive
- be the same as an existing trademark
- contain a 'sensitive' word or expression
- suggest a connection with government or local authorities without permission

the registration process

A sole trader must register with HM Revenue & Customs by 5th October following the end of the tax year in which they started in business.

Registration can be completed online by visiting www.hmrc.gov.uk. The details asked for are:

- national insurance number

- contact details

- date of registration

- unique tax reference (UTR) if a self-assessment tax return has been completed in the past

the tax return

Once registration has been completed, the sole trader will receive a UTR number and a self-assessment tax return must be completed each tax year.

The tax year runs from the 6th April to the following 5th April. The tax return must be submitted online by the following 31st January in order to avoid penalties.

If the tax return is submitted in the paper format, the deadline is 31st October following the end of the tax year.

Class 2 national insurance must be paid from the date the business commenced; it is due by 31st January following the end of the tax year.

Income tax and class 4 national insurance is calculated according to profits and must be paid by 31st January following the end of the tax year.

sole trader example

Daisy started in business as a beautician on 6th April 2021.

The first tax year that Daisy must submit a tax return for is 2021/22 (6th April 2021 to 5th April 2022).

She must register with HMRC by 5th October 2022.

Daisy must submit the tax return by 31st October 2022 if she chooses to complete a paper based return, or 31st January 2023 if the return is submitted online.

The income tax and national insurance due must be paid by 31st January 2023.

the tax and accounting records that must be kept

From the date that a sole trader started in business the following information must be kept:

- a record of all business income and expenditure, which can be in a manual or digital form
- details of any interest received, both business and personal
- details of any dividends received
- details of any other income received, for example rental income
- any amounts paid to personal pension schemes
- amounts paid under the Gift Aid scheme
- child benefit received
- details of student loans

All business records must be kept for 5 years and 10 months from the end of tax year.

sole trader example

Daisy must keep business records for the 2021/22 tax year until 31st January 2028.

business expenditure

The type of business expenditure will vary according to the kind of work carried out by the sole trader. Examples include:

purchase of goods for resale	telephone	repairs and tools
capital items – such as motor vehicles and equipment	insurance	professional fees
motor expenses	advertising	computer expenditure
staff wages (not those of the sole trader)	stationery	subscriptions

SETTING UP A BUSINESS AS A PARNERSHIP

The processes for setting up a partnership are very similar to those of a sole trader in terms of :

- the business name
- the registration process
- the tax and accounting records

the tax return

A partnership must register with HMRC under self-assessment and complete an annual self-assessment tax return for the partnership.

The individual partners must also register for self-assessment and complete their own individual self-assessment tax returns.

Both income tax and national insurance are payable on each partner's share of their profits.

Partners are jointly responsible for the filing of the partnership self-assessment tax return and registering for VAT if the VAT registration limit is reached.

HMRC must be informed if there is any change to the existing partnership (ie a partner joins or leaves).

partnership agreement

Partnerships must follow the rules of the Partnership Act 1890 and any partnership agreement (written or verbal) which has been drawn up by the partners.

A partnership agreement will include details on how profits and losses are divided between partners and their rights and responsibilities.

If no agreement exists then profits and losses must be shared equally between all partners in accordance with the Act.

SETTING UP A BUSINESS AS A LIMITED COMPANY

Companies are regulated by Companies House.

Companies House is a government body that stores information on all the limited companies and limited liability partnerships registered in the UK.

the business name

When deciding on a name for a new company, the name cannot be the same as another registered company's name.

The name must usually end in either 'Limited' or 'Ltd'.

Companies House have a company name availability checker, which can be used to identify whether or not a name can be used.

The name of the limited company must be shown on official paperwork.

Limited company names must not:

- include 'same as' names, where the only difference to an existing name is:
  - punctuation
  - special characters
  - a word or character that is similar in appearance or meaning
- be too similar to another company's name or existing trademark; it may have to be changed if a complaint is made
- be offensive
- contain a 'sensitive' word or expression
- suggest a connection with government or local authorities without permission

A limited company can trade using a different name to the registered name. This is known as a business name.

the registration process – Companies House

In order to set up a private limited company, there is a requirement to register with Companies House the following details:

- company name
- address of the registered office
- the details of a minimum of one director
- details of the shareholders, again a minimum of one (who may be the same individual as the director)
- details of the share capital (the number, value and type)
- a memorandum of association and articles of association

Companies House will charge a small fee for the incorporation process.

If the company is approved, Companies House will issue a certificate of incorporation with the date of incorporation and the company number.

Individuals may choose to purchase an off-the-shelf company rather than completing the registration process.

Some further explanations are provided below:

■ **memorandum of association** - a legal statement signed by all initial shareholders agreeing to form the company

■ **articles of association** - these set out the basic rules for the running of the company

■ **off-the-shelf companies** - these are companies that have already been registered with Companies House but have never traded. They can be purchased for a cost and are available to use immediately

■ The **share capital** of a company is divided into a number of shares which may be:

– ordinary shares - these shares entitle the shareholder to voting rights, and distributions (dividends) are based on how well the company performs

– preference shares - theses share will usually carry no voting rights; the dividends will usually be paid at a fixed percentage and are paid before any payments to ordinary shareholders

the registration process – HMRC

The company must register with HM Revenue & Customs (HMRC) within three months of the date the company starts to trade.

Registration can be completed after the UTR (unique tax reference) has been received (by post), with the following details:

■ company number

■ the date trading commenced

■ annual accounting date

A company can choose any accounting (year-end) date, for example 31 January, 30 April, 31 August etc. Often the choice of a 31 March year-end date can simplify calculations, as it falls in line with the financial year.

filing

Limited companies need to pay corporation tax each year on the company's profits to HMRC.

The deadline for paying corporation tax depends on the company's financial year-end.

The annual accounts for the financial year must be filed with Companies House nine months after the year-end date (six months for a public limited company) (plc).

Any corporation tax due for this financial year must be paid within nine months and one day of the year-end date.

Companies must also file a company tax return with HMRC by twelve months of the year-end date.

Most small limited companies find it more efficient to file their annual accounts to Companies House and their company tax return to HMRC at the same time.

Filing to both Companies House and HMRC is electronic only.

All companies must submit a **confirmation statement** to Companies House

The confirmation statement provides basic information about the company such as the registered office, directors, shareholders, contact details and the nature of the business. Do not confuse the confirmation statement with the company's annual accounts and tax return – they are completely separate and will not usually be filed at the same time. The confirmation statement is usually due around the time of year that the company was incorporated.

limited company example

Daisy Ltd has a financial year-end of 31st March 2022.

The financial statements must be filed electronically with Companies House by 31st December 2022.

Any corporation tax due must be paid to HMRC by 1st January 2023.

The corporation tax return must be submitted to HMRC by 31st March 2023.

the records that must be kept

Limited companies must keep certain records about the company, known as the **statutory books**. These include:

- details of directors
- details of shareholders
- details of company secretaries (if there are any)
- promises for the company to repay loans at a specific date in the future ('debentures') and who they must be paid back to
- promises the company makes for payments if something goes wrong and it's the company's fault ('indemnities')
- transactions when someone buys shares in the company
- loans or mortgages secured against the company's assets
- details of student loans

The law relating to limited companies (Companies Act) requires that companies should keep the following **accounting records:**

- records of entries made of payments received and made by the company and a description of each entry

- a record of the assets (items owned) and liabilities (items owed)

- records of inventory held

For **taxation (HMRC)** purposes the financial records which have been used to prepare the financial statements and company tax return must be retained. These records include financial documents and books of account such as purchase orders, invoices, credit notes, cash book, petty cash book, contracts and bank statements.

retention of financial records

Financial records should be retained in an accessible form in case of future queries, or even future legal action against the company.

Companies normally have a retention policy stating that records are kept for six years, plus the current year. The reasons for this are based on law. Tax and company law generally require records to be kept for at least six years.

SETTING UP A BUSINESS AS AN LIMITED LIABILITY PARTNERSHIP (LLP)

LLPs are regulated by Companies House.

the business name

The same rules apply as those for limited companies, except the name must end with 'Limited Liability Partnership' or 'LLP'.

the registration process – Companies House

The process is similar to that of a company with the following details required:

- LLP name

- address of registered office

- the details of at least two members

- LLP agreement

the registration process – HMRC

The LLP will be automatically registered with HMRC once the business has been registered with Companies House.

Every member of an LLP must register with HMRC for self-assessment.

filing

Annual accounts must be filed with Companies House nine months after the year end date.

An annual self-assessment tax return for the LLP must be filed with HMRC and is due by 31st January following the end of the tax year.

Note: LLPs do not have their own tax liability.

Individual members of a LLP must file an annual self-assessment tax return with HMRC by 31st January following the end of the tax year, any income tax and national insurance payable is also due on this date.

retention of financial records

LLPs must keep financial records for three years after the date they were made.

Chapter Summary

- Law is a set of principles and regulations set by government.

- The UK Parliament passes legislation through Acts of Parliament.

- Case law is established through the courts system.

- Common law was established through local customs and case precedent.

- Equity introduced fairness into the English legal system.

- Criminal law relates to crime, civil law relates to a civil wrong.

- Public law relates to the relationships between individuals and the government, private law relates to relationships between individuals.

- European Union (EU) law took precedent over domestic law, some of which has been retained since Brexit.

- The three elements that are essential to all contracts are:

  - agreement

  - consideration

  - intention to create legal relations

- Contracts may be valid, void or voidable.

- If contract terms are broken there may be a breach of contract and legal action for damages may be sought.

- There are different rules and regulations that must be followed when setting up a business as a sole trader, partnership or limited company.

- Sole traders and partnerships must file self-assessment tax returns with HMRC.

- Companies must file corporation tax returns and accounts with HMRC and accounts with Companies House.

- Business records must be retained in a suitable format for a pre-determined length of time.

Key Terms		
	common law system	passing legislation and creating precedents through case law
	UK Parliament	consists of the King, the House of Commons and the House of Lords
	Act of Parliament	legislation which has been approved by a majority in the House of Commons and the House of Lords
	Bill	draft legislation
	Royal Assent	a Bill which has been formally approved by the King
	the courts system	ranges from County Courts to the UK Supreme Court, to hear court cases and establish case law
	judge	a public officer who is appointed to decide cases in law courts
	magistrate	a volunteer who hears court cases in their community
	jury	a group of individuals from the general public, who have been chosen to listen to the facts in a court case and to deliver a verdict of guilty or not guilty
	equity	allows a court to grant discretionary remedies
	claimant	an individual who has suffered a loss or injury
	defendant	an individual who has allegedly caused a loss or injury
	contract	a legally binding agreement which is enforceable in a court of law
	an agreement	comprising of offer and an acceptance
	consideration	value passing between two parties
	intention to create legal relations	a commercial agreement which could be taken to a court of law if the need arose
	invitation to treat	an invitation to an individual or business to make an offer
	breach of contract	breaking of the terms of a contract and grounds for taking legal action

memorandum of association   legal statement to agree to form a company

articles of association   sets out the basic rules for how a company is run

Companies House   the government body in the UK which stores information on companies

Activities

3.1   Which of the following does not approve Bills before they become an Act of Parliament?

(a)	House of Commons	
(b)	House of Lords	
(c)	the Lord Chief Justice	
(d)	the King	

3.2   A group of individuals who have been chosen to deliver a guilty or not guilty verdict in a court case are called:

(a)	Magistrates	
(b)	Jury	
(c)	Judges	
(d)	Panel members	

3.3   Within common law the only remedy is:

(a)	Injunction	
(b)	Rectification	
(c)	Damages	
(d)	Rescission	

3.4   Identify whether each of the following relate to criminal law or civil law:

		Criminal law	Civil law
(a)	Theft		
(b)	Breach of contract		
(c)	Negligence		
(d)	Terrorism		

3.5   Select which **two** of the following relate to public law:

(a)	contract law	
(b)	administrative law	
(c)	family law	
(d)	human rights law	

3.6   Consideration in a contract is:

(a)	Taking advice before entering into a contract	
(b)	The promise by both parties to exchange value	
(c)	The need for both parties to have capacity to contract	
(d)	The intention to create legal relations	

Which **one** of these options is correct?

3.7   Tracey shops for milk in a supermarket. A contract is formed when:

(a)	She ticks the milk off her shopping list	
(b)	She takes the milk off the shelf and puts it in her trolley	
(c)	She places the milk on the checkout conveyor belt	
(d)	The checkout assistant scans the milk and the price shows on the display	

Which **one** of these options is correct?

3.8   Maria agrees to do some cleaning for her friend, Carlo, as a favour. After she has done the work he promises to give her £10 because he is so pleased with it. This constitutes a valid contract.

True or False? State your reasons for your answer.

3.9 George looks at some new football boots on a website and sees that one pair is advertised at £37.99 'with 30% off'. He wants to purchase them. This price is:

(a)	Contractually binding	
(b)	An invitation to treat	
(c)	An example of specific performance	
(d)	An acceptance	

Which **one** of these options is correct?

3.10 A written contract that may be set aside because one of the parties was pressured into signing it is known as:

(a)	A void contract	
(b)	A voidable contract	
(c)	A valid contract	

Which **one** of these options is correct?

3.11 Select true or false for the following statements:

	True	False
(a) A sole trader must register with Companies House within three months of starting a business.		
(b) A partnership will always split profits equally between partners.		

3.12 List the details that an individual must have in order to register as a sole trader.

3.13 List the details that are required to set up a private limited company with Companies House.

4 The finance function

this chapter covers...

This chapter describes the role of the finance function in an organisation such as a business. It includes the various areas in which finance staff are likely to work and how they provide information for others, exploring the importance of effectiveness and efficiency.

The chapter explains the following in detail:

- *the key responsibilities of the finance function*

- *the difference between internal and external stakeholders*

- *the ways in which the finance function in an organisation provides information and support both to other departments in the organisation and also to outside stakeholders*

- *how basic accounting carried out by bookkeepers and accounts assistants involves a wide variety of areas – sales order processing, purchasing, cashiering, payroll, costing and stock control*

- *different roles and reporting lines within the finance function*

- *effective business relationships and communication*

- *efficient working practices in the finance function*

- *the importance of working capital and solvency*

- *policies and procedures relating to the finance function and wider organisation*

THE RESPONSIBILITIES OF THE FINANCE FUNCTION

The finance function of an organisation is the department that deals with financial transactions, accounting records, financial reports, management accounting, treasury management and in larger organisations, internal audit. It may sometimes be referred to as the accounts department.

the size of the finance function

In a very small business, the business owner may carry out the finance functions, alongside the running of the business, often with the support of an external accountant.

sole trader example

Rob is a sole trader, who runs a barbers' shop.

Rob uses a spreadsheet to record his daily takings and outgoings. He reconciles all bankings and card receipts to his bank statements. He makes regular trips to specialist suppliers to purchase products and equipment.

Once a quarter, Rob hands over his spreadsheets, bank statements and details of expenditure to an external accountant. The accountant prepares the quarterly VAT returns, year-end accounts and the self-assessment tax return for Rob.

Smaller businesses may have one dedicated finance person, or the role may be outsourced to a professional, for example bookkeepers or accountants.

small limited company example

Lily and Lilac Ltd is a flower shop which employs six members of staff. The day-to-day finance operations are outsourced to an external bookkeeper, Rose.

Rose uses accounting software to:

- enter all sales invoices and record income received

- match purchase orders to invoices received from suppliers, coding them appropriately and recording payments to suppliers once they have been approved by the business owners

- record all other expenditure

- reconcile the bank

- prepare quarterly VAT returns

- prepare monthly payroll

The statutory financial accounts and tax documentation are prepared by a firm of accountants, using the information supplied by Rose and the business owners.

Larger businesses will have many individuals or teams providing the financial functions of the business. Individuals or teams may have responsibilities for specific areas, such as:

- sales order processing

- purchasing

- bank account monitoring

- payroll

- management accounting

- inventory control

the finance function and stakeholders

The finance function within an organisation provides a service to other people both internally and externally. These people are known as **stakeholders**. The finance function provide information, support, advice and guidance to stakeholders.

A stakeholder of an organisation is an individual, a group of people or another organisation that has an interest or connection with the organisation and is affected by what it does.

external stakeholders

Set out below are examples of **external stakeholders** for Lily and Lilac Ltd, the flower shop:

- **shareholders** – individual owners of the company who receive dividend payments paid out of profits made by the company; they may also have a role in managing the company

- **banks** who lend money and provide other forms of finance; they will require financial projections of cash and profit to indicate whether or not repayments can be made

- **customers** who depend on the business for good quality products and customer service at a reasonable price; customers may also have an expectation that the business should support sustainability (such as, supporting charity, the local community and energy saving)

- **suppliers** who sell to the company, who want to see that it is financially sound and will regularly pay its bills

- **regulatory bodies**, eg the UK Financial Reporting Council, which requires that the company's accounts are properly prepared and accurately reported to stakeholders

■ **government bodies** and **agencies** (for example HM Revenue & Customs, Companies House and the Department of Trade and Industry).

The relationship between a finance function and external stakeholders is illustrated below.

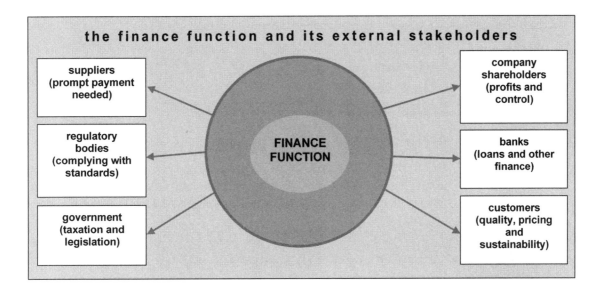

the finance function and its external stakeholders

suppliers
(prompt payment
needed)

regulatory
bodies
(complying with
standards)

government
(taxation and
legislation)

FINANCE
FUNCTION

company
shareholders
(profits and
control)

banks
(loans and other
finance)

customers
(quality, pricing
and
sustainability)

the finance function – internal support

Whatever the size of a business, the finance function will carry out a variety of tasks to help keep the business running. The finance function will treat the people or departments within the business it is supporting as **internal stakeholders**, because they rely on the finance function for support. Without the involvement of the finance function, the business would not be able to continue operating.

The main operating areas of the finance function are as follows:

■ **sales order processing** – taking sales orders, producing invoices, monitoring receipts – all the jobs connected with the receivables ledger

■ **purchasing** – sending out orders, checking the incoming documentation, making payments – all the jobs connected with the payables ledger

■ **bank account monitoring** – recording income and expenditure and dealing with cash held in the business – all the jobs connected with bank transactions and petty cash

■ **payroll** – maintaining payroll records, calculating the payroll and processing payroll payments

Other specialist finance jobs include:

■ **management accounting** – working out the figures for the cost of products and services, forecasting future receipts and payments and preparing reports for management

■ **inventory control** – monitoring and re-ordering inventory

In Chapter 1 we considered other business functions that a business may have within its structure, such as:

■ operations

■ sales and marketing

■ human resources

■ information technology

■ distribution and logistics

In the diagram below, the white boxes show individual areas of the finance function and the remaining text shows how they can support various functions of a business.

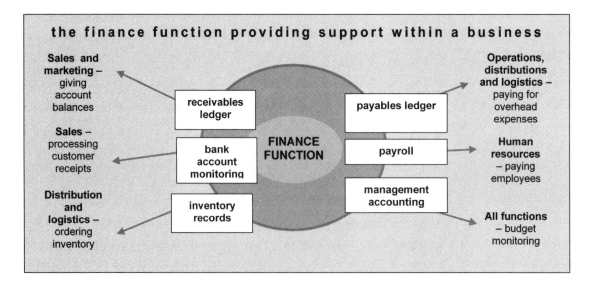

examples of information provided by the finance function

■ the receivables ledger section can keep sales staff updated with the credit status of their customers, highlighting any slow payers

■ the payables ledger section can advise the operations, distributions and logistics departments of how much is owed to suppliers for purchases and overhead expenses

- the payroll section can advise the human resources department about payroll costs, for example how much overtime was paid last month

- the management accounting section can advise the operations department of the direct costs of production (for example, materials) and also the overhead costs of production (for example rent and depreciation)

financial statements

In Chapter 1 we considered the content of the financial statements for sole traders, partnerships and companies.

In small businesses, such as the examples of Rob, the sole trader and Lily and Lilac Ltd, external accountants will prepare the financial statements.

Larger companies may use financial accountants in house to prepare the financial statements, or they may also use external accountants for this purpose. However, for a limited company the overall responsibility for the preparation of the financial statements lies with the directors.

DIFFERENT ROLES WITHIN THE FINANCE FUNCTION

bookkeepers, finance assistants and trainees

Bookkeepers, finance assistants and trainees carry out the day-to-day financial functions of businesses. This may include operating the receivables and payables ledgers, recording income and expenditure from bank, cash and other payments methods, such as PayPal and credit cards.

accountants

Accountants form the next level up from assistants and trainees. They include:

- financial accountants

- management accountants

- auditors

financial accountants

The function of the **financial accountant** is concerned with financial transactions, and uses the information produced by the bookkeeper or accounts assistant. The financial accountant extracts information from the accounting records in order to provide a method of control, for example, over customers who buy on credit, over suppliers, cash and bank balances. The role of a financial accountant also involves the analysis and reporting of financial data so that financial statements can be prepared.

management accountants

The **management accountant** obtains information about costs (for example, the cost of labour, materials, expenses (overheads)), interprets the data and prepares reports and budgets for the owners or managers of the business. The management accountant is concerned with financial decision-making, planning and control of the business.

auditors

Auditors are accountants whose role is to check that accounting procedures have been followed correctly. There are two types of auditors: **external auditors** and **internal auditors**.

External auditors are independent of the business whose accounts are being audited. They are normally members of firms of accountants. The most common type of audit conducted by external auditors is the audit of larger limited companies. This is a legal requirement. The examples of financial statements from Sainsburys and Tesco include reports from the external auditors:

- https://about.sainsburys.co.uk/investors/results-reports-and-presentations/2021

- https://www.tescoplc.com/investors/reports-results-and-presentations/annual-report-2021/

Internal auditors are employed or contracted by the business which they audit. Their duties are concerned with the internal check and control procedures of the business, for example monitoring the procedures for the control of cash, and the authorisation of purchases.

REPORTING LINES WITHIN THE FINANCE FUNCTION

All businesses are different and the structure and size of the finance function will differ from business to business.

the organisational structure of the business

The following example shows the organisational structure of a business and is based on the finance roles in a company. The boxes with the dark grey background all represent finance roles. You will see that the structure is set out in a series of layers of authority and responsibility. This type of structure is known as a '**hierarchy**' – the lowest level includes the accounts assistants, and as you move up the structure, the people involved gain both power and responsibility.

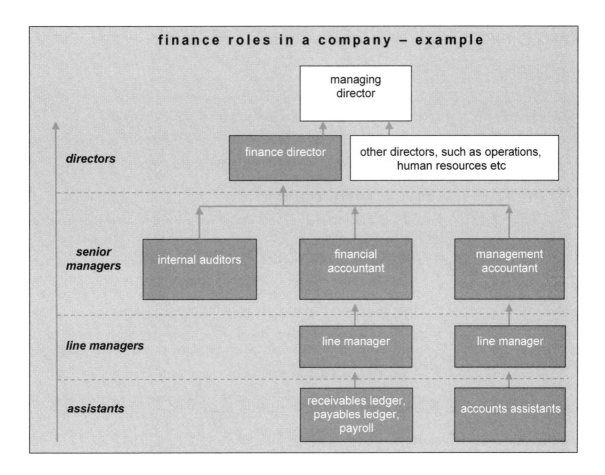

reporting lines between levels

The arrows in the diagram represent 'up and down' **reporting lines** within the organisation. A reporting line means that the people lower down in the structure always report to the next layer up. In the example, accounts assistants report to line managers, who in turn report to the senior managers, who in turn report to the directors.

For example, a person within a lower level role is able to pass on to a person in higher level role:

- specific information that is required or has been requested

- regular reports that are needed

- day-to-day work for approval and authorisation

- complaints about the work, work conditions or colleagues

- suggestions about how to improve the way the work is organised

It follows that people with higher role levels in the company have the authority to:

- request information

- commission reports

- approve and authorise work carried out at the lower level

- deal with complaints and resolve the issue (or pass it to the next level up)

- organise discussions about the way the work is organised

other reporting lines

In addition to the formal 'up and down' reporting lines described, there are other identifiable reporting lines within an organisation. These include:

- people **on the same level** of authority, possibly working in a different section of the same department and regularly providing information and reports, for example, a payroll assistant providing details to the cashier to make the payments to employees for their wages

- people **on a different level** of authority who are reported to for a specific function within the organisation, for example, an accounts assistant:

  - reporting to a training manager to have a talk about training needs

  - reporting as a representative of the finance department, who is elected to the company social responsibility committee to decide on a charitable cause to support

EFFECTIVE BUSINESS RELATIONSHIPS IN FINANCE

the meaning of 'effective' working

The word 'effective' means:

being successful in achieving what you set out to do.

If an organisation is to work effectively, smoothly and without any hitches, it is important that the finance function operates efficiently. This means that the management of the organisation must ensure that:

- finance tasks must be carefully checked by a more senior person – for example, the issue of a sales invoice and the preparation of payroll

- finance tasks must be authorised – for example, the approval for payment of a purchase invoice and processing of payroll

- any problems with any accounting system should be reported to a higher authority

- requests for information or a report should be clear and a realistic timescale indicated

For a finance function in an organisation to be successful and 'effective' it needs to establish good working relationships:

- **internally** – with members of the finance 'team' and also with other functions of the business, for example other departments such as sales and marketing and operations

- **externally** – for example, with customers and suppliers

internal business relationships

It is important for any team such as a finance function to achieve its goals by respecting and building positive relations with work colleagues:

- in the **finance function**; this involves

  - complying with the requests of managers promptly

  - complying with the requests of other work colleagues

  - working according to defined work procedures

  - helping out work colleagues when you think help is needed, for example if they are stressed out with too much work or if they are new to the job and need guidance and reassurance

- carrying out requests for information from **other functions** (departments), for example:

  - complying with the requests of managers from other departments, for example, financial reports needed for a meeting

  - providing regular information to other functions, for example, sales figures to the sales and marketing function

If members of the finance function are not prepared to comply with these types of request promptly and positively, both the finance function and the whole business can be affected in a negative way. This will have consequences not only for the finance function but also the whole business, its relations with its stakeholders, and particularly with its customers.

external business relationships

It is equally important for the finance function to ensure that it promotes a good working relationship with its customers and other external stakeholders.

Customers like to be treated promptly, with courtesy and provided with information that is accurate. This will give the business a good reputation which means that the customer is likely to recommend it to others.

If the customers of a business are happy, it means that the staff who deal with the customers are also likely to be happy and motivated. A happy customer is also a loyal customer and a loyal customer helps to maintain the sales income and ultimately the profit of the business.

EFFECTIVE COMMUNICATION

communication in general

If you are communicating a message to another person or group of people, that message must be **effective.** It must achieve its aim and be:

- clear and easily understood

- concise – not too long-winded

- unambiguous, using straightforward language so that the meaning cannot be misinterpreted

- complete – the whole message must be there

- accurate – there is no point in unintentionally misleading people

- provided at the right time – not too early and not too late (timely)

- appropriate to the person or people receiving it and to meet their needs

- in the most appropriate format (medium), whether by phone, message, email, letter or report

On a personal level, if you are organising a meal out with a group of friends, you will need to email, phone or text instructions giving clear details of the place, date and time and asking for confirmation.

You need to provide all this information in good time to the right people and be available to receive replies. You need to make sure the instructions are very clear otherwise the meal could turn out to be a non-event.

This is a very basic comparison, but the same principles apply to any workplace situation.

workplace communication

Communication can be very varied. If you think about a working day and compile a list of all the forms of communication you get involved in, you would find that you would be recording:

- **internal communications** – with colleagues, line managers and anyone else involved in your reporting lines

- **external communications** – depending on your role in the organisation, this could be with customers, suppliers, or financial institutions

If you are communicating **within the organisation** you should

- choose the most appropriate method

- be polite – even if you do not feel like it at the time

- act promptly – do not leave things to later, they may never happen

If you are communicating **externally** you should

- choose the most appropriate method of communication

- communicate clearly, accurately and promptly

- present a professional approach

- comply with 'corporate image' – this may mean using standard letters and emails, or speaking on the telephone using standard 'scripts'

The need to develop effective business communication skills is covered in Chapter 6 of this book.

EFFICIENT WORKING PRACTICES IN FINANCE

the need for efficiency

'Efficiency' can be described as:

'achieving the right result with the minimum of wasted time, effort or expense.'

Efficiency is an important objective for any organisation.

The information provided by the finance function should be:

- **complete** – all the information needed is provided

- **accurate** – the information must be 100% correct

- **on time** – the information should be provided within the given timescale

If these three conditions are fulfilled by the staff working in accounting and finance roles, it contributes to the **efficiency** of the organisation, its smooth running and its profitability.

achieving efficiency in the finance function

There are various ways in which efficiency in the finance function can be maintained and improved:

- by the **individual employee**:
  - treating other employees and management with respect
  - taking pride in the tasks performed and making sure that the accounting procedures are fully understood
  - ensuring all systems are understood and are up to date
  - carrying out tasks that are within their capability

- by the **employer**:
  - treating employees with respect and encouraging motivation
  - ensuring that accounting procedures are followed properly
  - arranging appropriate training so that each employee's job is done properly and expertly
  - ensuring that there are sufficient staff to cover the required finance tasks
  - making sure the staff work appropriate hours and are paid an appropriate wage for their level of work
  - ensuring that the business remains solvent (see below)
  - making sure the business has long term financial stability
  - ensuring that all relevant legal requirements are understood and followed (see Chapter 3)
  - making sure that the business is fully compliant with any regulations that are specific to the business or the sector that it operates in.

the need for solvency

'Solvency' means being able to pay your debts when they are due.

You are 'solvent' when you can pay your debts and 'insolvent' when you cannot.

For a business organisation – for example, a chain of shops, a bank or a football club – the inability to pay debts when they are due means that the business has become **insolvent**. This can result in court action, closure of the business and the loss of jobs. It also means that suppliers who are owed money are likely to lose most or all of what they are owed.

How does all this relate to the efficiency of the finance function of an organisation such as a business?

A business needs to know that it will have enough money in the bank to be able to pay its debts. This means that the finance function will have to provide accurate and complete information to management about:

- how much money it has **at present**

- how much money it will have coming in and going out **in the future**

Specifically it will need to know accurate details of:

money in:

- the balance of money in the bank account

- amounts coming in from customers and when they are due

money out:

- amounts due to suppliers and for other expenses, such as payroll and rent, and when they are due

This can be calculated by the business producing a forecast known as a **cash budget**, which can assist in identifying predicted shortfalls and surpluses in cash.

The cash budget is introduced to your studies at Level 3 Management Accounting Techniques.

cash budget example

Cash budget for Lilac and Lily Ltd for the period ended 31 March 20-1:

	January £	February £	March £
Receipts:			
Sales	19,500	19,600	19,650
Bank loan	-	-	25,000
Total receipts	**19,500**	**19,600**	**44,650**
Payments:			
Purchases	4,250	5,750	5,000
Shop refit	-	28,000	-
Operating expenses	3,600	3,600	3,600
Wages	8,800	8,800	8,800
Total payments	**16,650**	**46,150**	**17,400**
Net cash flow	**2,850**	**(26,550)**	**27,250**
Opening bank / (overdraft)	**5,860**	**8.710**	**(17,840)**
Closing bank / (overdraft)	**8,710**	**(17,840)**	**9,410**

The example shown is the cash budget for Lilac and Lily Ltd for the three months to 31 March 20-1.

The cash budget shows:

- the balance of money in the bank account at the start of January, £5,860

- the expected income and payments for each of the three months

- the difference between the income and payments for each of the three months (the net cash flow)

- the balance of money in the bank account at the end of each month

Lilac and Lily Ltd are expecting to carry out a shop refit in February for £28,000. This will mean that the bank will go into overdraft at the end of February by £17,840. The directors of Lily and Lilac Ltd have arranged for a bank loan in March for £25,000 so that the bank account will no longer be overdrawn.

the need for working capital and being solvent

The surplus of:

- money in, money due and money that can be quickly realised over

- money due to be paid out

is known as **working capital**.

As long as 'money in, money due in and money realisable' is greater than 'money to be paid out', working capital is positive and the business **can pay its debts when they are due**, therefore it is **solvent**.

Careful management of working capital by the finance function is very important if the business is to remain solvent. There are some basic rules to observe:

- pay money into the bank account as soon as possible; do not leave it for a long time before processing it

- negotiate credit periods with your suppliers

- make sure your credit customers pay on time and try and keep the payment terms as short as possible, for example 30 days rather than 90 days

Problems can arise when there is less money coming in than going out. A new business can sometimes run into trouble, for example, if it does not manage its working capital efficiently, as the following Case Study shows.

**Case
Study**

JIMMY CASH: WORKING CAPITAL AND SOLVENCY

situation

Jimmy Cash has recently started business importing home alarm systems. He has put £25,000 of his savings into the bank and negotiated with four main suppliers who have asked for payment of their invoices within 30 days.

Jimmy has been phoning around to sell his products to shops and mail order firms. He is pleased with the response, although a number of his customers have asked for payment terms of 60 days, saying that 'You will have to give me 60 days if you want the business'.

Sales for the first three months go well and Jimmy has taken on two new employees to deal with the volume of orders received. Things have been so busy in this period that Jimmy has been unable to get to the bank very often to pay in some cash that he has received from customers. He has received calls from two of his suppliers chasing payment of their invoices and threatening cutting off supplies if he does not pay up. He is also aware that some of his customers have not settled their first invoices.

At the end of the three months he gets a call from the bank asking him to call them to discuss his bank account which is now £5,000 overdrawn.

Jimmy asks for your help and advice.

solution

You tell Jimmy that he is in a dangerous situation because he has not managed his working capital properly and may be insolvent. He may not be able to settle his debts (to the bank and his suppliers) from the money coming in from his sales to customers.

You advise Jimmy

- to request the bank to allow him to pay off the overdraft over the next six months or convert the overdraft into a loan
- to chase up any customers who are late paying and to bank the cash
- to try and negotiate a longer payment period from his suppliers
- to regularly monitor his bank balance and prepare a cash budget

summary

Jimmy has basically ignored the need for careful cash management, and despite running a successful business, is in immediate danger of becoming insolvent.

ORGANISATIONAL POLICIES AND PROCEDURES

Organisational policies and procedures are often set down in a series of procedures manuals which should be updated regularly and readily available for reference by employees.

policies and procedures for the finance function

Some of the principles set out in the procedures manuals for the finance function will be established in law, the details of which were included in Chapter 3.

An example extract from an internal policies and procedures document for a finance function is set out on the next page.

Each employee within the finance function is placed within a certain level of authority and will report to a higher level who will be given the responsibility of **authorising** whatever it is that the more junior employee is required to do. Typical transactions and documents which require authorisation include:

- authorisation of purchases (the signing of purchase orders)

- the making of payments (signing BACS payment orders)

- paying in at the bank (signing the paying in slip)

- petty cash payments (signing the petty cash voucher)

- payroll processing (checking and signing the payment instructions)

If the organisation is a large one, the authorisation process may be more complex. For example:

- authorising payments up to £1,000 may require one signature, whereas payments of £1,000 or more may require two signatures

- authorisation of payroll payments may require a senior manager's signature

If, however, it is a small business organisation, like Lilac and Lily Ltd, with only six employees, there will be far fewer regulations. The business owner will authorise everything and will delegate during periods of absence.

The important point to note is that employees should:

- know what needs authorising and by whom

- keep to the regulations with no short-cuts being taken

The organisation will then run far more efficiently and smoothly. If there are any problems or errors, the person responsible can be identified and the problem resolved and the errors corrected.

finance policies and procedures example

Accounting records

Proper accounting records will be kept. The accounts systems is based around computer facilities, using the accounting software and spreadsheets, but manual/paper records will also be used if appropriate. The following records will be kept:

- Appropriate control accounts (bank control, petty cash control, VAT control, payroll control)

- Monthly trial balances

- Petty cash and bank accounts will be reconciled at least monthly

- VAT returns produced on the required quarterly cycle

Ordering supplies and services

Budget holders can place orders for goods or services within their budget areas, subject only to cash flow restraints. All orders of £1,000 or more must be authorised by the budget holder, except for specific areas of expenditure where written procedures have been agreed. Under £1,000, the budget holder may delegate all ordering as appropriate. Budget holders will discuss with the Financial Controller appropriate parameters, plus maximum allowed deviations before the budget holder or senior manager is brought in, which will be documented.

Payment authorisation and payables ledger

All invoices must be authorised for payment by the budget holder, although the actual checking of details may be delegated. The authorising department is responsible for checking invoices for accuracy in terms of figures and conformity with the order placed, that the services or goods have been received, and following up any problems. Finance must be informed if there are queries delaying authorisation or if payment is to be withheld for any reason.

A payables ledger is operated by finance. All incoming invoices are to be passed to the finance section as soon as they arrive. Invoices will be recorded in the payables ledger within two days unless there are coding problems. They are then passed on to budget holders for authorisation. Once authorised, suppliers will be paid within the appropriate timescale.

Making payments and signing

Signatories will only be drawn from senior staff and directors, and any new signatory must be approved by the directors before the bank is notified. All amounts for £1,000 or over require two signatories. Signatories should check that the expenditure has been authorised by the appropriate person before payment is made. Salary payments require the signature of the Accounts Manager or Financial Controller, plus one other. The usual payment method will be BACS. If cheques are used, they should be filled in completely (with payee, amount in words and figures, and date) before they are signed.

Handling of cash

Petty cash will be topped up using the 'imprest' system, where the amount spent is reimbursed. It is intended for small items, up to £20. Anything over this should be paid through the bank where possible. The imprest has a balance limit of £250. The petty cash balance will be reconciled when restoring the imprest balance, or monthly if this is more frequent. All cash collected from finance will be signed for, and receipts will be issued for all cash returned.

policies and procedures for the wider organisation

An efficient organisation will have well-established and documented policies and procedures covering a wide range of issues relating to staff behaviour and working practices. These are documented in procedures manuals which should be read by all staff in all areas of the business. These may include:

■ **code of conduct** – covering issues such as the use of the internet and emails, mobile phones, drug and alcohol policy

A code of conduct will define acceptable and unacceptable staff behaviour. An efficient business will not tolerate behaviour which will disrupt the normal workflow, as in the following two cases:

code of conduct example

No employee is to start work or return to work whilst under the influence of alcohol or drugs. A breach of this policy is grounds for disciplinary action, up to and including termination of employment.

Using the organisation's computer resources to seek out, access or send any material of an offensive, obscene or defamatory nature is prohibited and may result in disciplinary action.

Harsh rules, however, do not always increase efficiency. Some employers allow the personal use of the internet or mobile phones in employees' free time at work and find that this improves employees' work rate and efficiency.

■ **health and safety** – maintaining a safe and hazard-free working environment

Responsibility for health and safety in the workplace lies both with the **employee** and the **employer**. You should be aware that there are many different laws governing this area, the most well-known of which is the **Health and Safety at Work Act**. You do not need to know the detail of these laws but you should be aware of the principles. Their aims are:

– to ensure that health and safety measures are introduced and observed both by employers and employees

– to specify the rights and responsibilities of employers and employees

– to enable employees to obtain compensation in the case of injury or ill health caused by conditions in the workplace

A health and safety policy is likely to contain:

– the names of the people responsible for health and safety

– the need for safety when employees operate machinery, handle unsafe substances or lift heavy objects

– the need and procedures for employees to report accidents, serious illnesses or fatalities in the workplace

– the forms needed (including copies) for reporting accidents and hazards

If organisations are to be efficient and well run they should avoid:

– electrical hazards – trailing leads and cables

– blockages and obstacles – filing drawers left open, waste bins in the way, boxes stacked up in corridors

– fire doors wedged open (ie safety doors that normally swing shut)

– employees taking unnecessary risks – standing on chairs and desks, lifting items that are too heavy or not bending properly when lifting

– using a computer workstation and not taking regular breaks or not using suitable seating

■ **corporate ethics** – guidelines on issues such as honesty, integrity and customer focus

■ **confidentiality** – ensuring security and privacy of customer data

■ **sustainability policies** – saving the planet through conservation of energy and recycling

■ **corporate social responsibility** – protection of the environment, helping society and improving the welfare of the workforce

Ethics, confidentiality, sustainability and corporate social responsibility are covered in detail in Chapter 8.

Chapter Summary

■ The **finance function** is a term which describes the work carried out by the finance department of an organisation such as a business.

■ A **stakeholder** is a group of people or another organisation that has an interest or connection with the organisation and is affected by what it does.

■ The finance function deals with **external stakeholders** such as the shareholders of a company, banks, customers, suppliers, government and regulatory bodies.

■ The finance function deals with **internal stakeholders** by supplying support to other people and departments within the business.

■ The main operating areas of the finance function include:

– sales order processing

– purchasing

– bank account monitoring

– payroll

– management accounting

– inventory control

■ **Bookkeepers, finance assistants** and **trainees** perform the day-to-day operations of the finance function.

■ **Accountants** have responsibility for various areas of the finance function, including the recording of financial information, financial reporting, forecasting, planning and managing.

■ **Financial accountants** deal with the reporting of past financial transactions and their presentation in financial statements for internal and external use.

■ **Management accountants** provide past and projected financial data to managers so that forward planning can take place in the form of budgets, and decisions made about the use of resources.

■ **Auditors** are accountants whose role it is to check that accounting procedures have been followed correctly. Internal auditors are employees of the organisation and look over its accounting systems; external auditors are independent firms of accountants who verify the accounts.

■ A **reporting line** is the direct relationship between a manager and the people who work under them. It involves the passing of information, suggestions and complaints. Well-developed reporting lines are essential in any well-run organisation, especially larger organisations.

■ The finance function is responsible for providing **financial statements.**

■ **Effective working** in an organisation means the organisation is successful in what it sets out to do.

■ An important aspect of effective working in the finance function of a business means being successful in establishing **good working relationships**. These relationships should not only be with customers and other external stakeholders but also internally within the finance function and with other departments.

■ **Communication** within an organisation and with outsiders must be effective to be successful. This means it must be clear, concise, accurate and delivered on time. It must also be in the most appropriate format.

■ **Efficiency** in an organisation means achieving the right result with the minimum of wasted time, effort or expense. Efficiency is an important objective of effective working.

■ **Solvency** means being able to pay debts when they are due. If there is a shortage of cash there is a risk of insolvency. The finance function must monitor and control the cash position to prevent the cash from running out.

■ **Policies and procedures** are internal documents which regulate a wide variety of areas of the business. Each function will have its own policies and procedures.

finance function	the department of an organisation that deals with financial transactions, accounting records, financial reports, management accounting, treasury management and audit
stakeholder	a person, group of people or another organisation that has an interest in the performance of an organisation
internal stakeholder	a section of an organisation which relies on another part of the business for information and support
external stakeholder	a person, group of people or organisation outside an organisation that has an interest in its performance
accounting	the process of recording, analysing and reporting financial information
financial accounting	the analysis and reporting of past financial transactions in financial reports
management accounting	providing past and projected financial information for managers to help with planning, decision making and control
internal auditing	internal checking of the financial records by an employee of the organisation
external auditing	external checking of the financial records by independent accountants
effective working	being successful in what you set out to do
efficiency	achieving the right result with the minimum of wasted time, effort or expense
solvency	being able to repay your debts when they are due
policies and procedures	rules and regulations to be followed within an organisation for the running of defined areas of activity

Activities

4.1   The most appropriate description of the finance function in an organisation is:

(a)	It is limited to cash handling and the raising of finance	
(b)	It is limited to financial records and financial reports	
(c)	It deals with financial records, financial reports and customer marketing	
(d)	It deals with cash, financial records, financial reports, costing and budgets	

Tick the **one** correct option.

4.2   Indicate with a tick which of the following would be considered an external stakeholder of a limited company:

(a)	HM Revenue & Customs	
(b)	The board of directors of the company	
(c)	The company's bank	
(d)	The customers of the business	
(e)	The employees of the business	
(f)	The suppliers of the business	

4.3   A financial accountant is a person who:

(a)	Prepares the financial statements of a business	
(b)	Sets budgets for the next financial year	
(c)	Checks the accounting procedures used within a business	

Tick the **one** correct option.

4.4 Complete the following sentence by using the correct terms set out in bold print below.

external auditor   **internal auditor**

An [   ] is normally an employee of the organisation being

audited, but an [   ] should be a member of an independent

firm of accountants.

4.5 The meaning of effective working is as follows:

(a)	Being successful in achieving what you set out to do	
(b)	Completing what you have to do as soon as possible	
(c)	Creating the maximum effect in order to improve performance	
(d)	Always complying with the requests of colleagues	

4.6 Which **one** of the following is the most accurate definition of efficiency?

(a)	To complete a job as quickly as possible at all costs	
(b)	To complete a job with the minimum of wasted time, effort or expense	
(c)	To complete a job exactly as described in the Policies and Procedures	
(d)	To complete a job using the cheapest way of doing it	

4.7 Which **two** of the following are qualities of an effective communication?

(a)	It needs to be made as quickly as possible	
(b)	It must be made within an appropriate timescale	
(c)	It needs to be made using language appropriate to the situation	
(d)	It needs to be made using formal and complex business language	

4.8 The policies and procedures for the finance function are likely to include:

(a)	Details of the authorisation needed for business purchases	
(b)	Details of annual appraisals of finance staff	
(c)	Records of customer names and addresses	
(d)	Passwords for all the computers in the business	

4.9 Which of the following is the most accurate definition of solvency of a business?

(a)	Receiving all customer payments on the due date	
(b)	Having a lot of money in the bank	
(c)	Being able to pay all company debts when they are due	
(d)	Delaying paying money into the bank as soon as it is received	

4.10 If a business wants to improve its working capital position, it should:

(a)	Pay suppliers earlier	
(b)	Get customers to pay earlier	
(c)	Pay employees' wages earlier	
(d)	Pay money in at the bank less frequently	

4.11 The diagram below shows the organisational structure of an accounts department in a small business which buys and sells goods on credit and pays employees weekly in cash.

Study the diagram and answer the questions that follow.

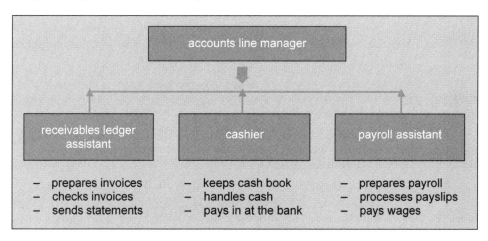

(a) Identify the three reporting lines in the diagram.

(b) Which assistant would the line manager ask if they wanted a report on customers who were bad payers?

(c) What other assistant level accounting roles might also feature in this diagram, which shows a business that buys and sells goods on credit?

5 Financial information and data security

this chapter covers...

This chapter illustrates the importance of information, the definitions of primary and secondary sources of information and how to establish whether or not information sources are valid.

Information and documents received within the finance function are covered and those which are internally produced by the finance function for management for decision making are included.

People working in the finance function must appreciate that the information, documents and data they use must be stored safely and securely.

This will be made possible by:

- *restricting access by using suitable passwords*
- *ensuring that all financial data and documents are regularly backed up and stored*
- *following the key principles of General Data Protection Regulation (GDPR)*
- *understanding the importance of cyber security*

INFORMATION

what is information?

We live in a world where information is everywhere, for example on our phones, electronic devices, when we travel, in various forms of media, in the workplace, schools and colleges and in the activities we carry out in our leisure time.

Information is the knowledge that is gained from an **investigation, a study or an instruction.**

For example:

- information on train times can be found by searching the internet (investigation)

- information on how to pass an exam can be found by attending a training course or reading material and practising questions (study)

- information on how to pay and order a takeaway can be achieved by reading a menu and making selections (instruction)

valid and invalid information

Information can be obtained from a vast array of sources. However, just because it is available does not mean that it is accurate and up to date.

Valid information can be obtained from reputable sources, such as HMRC, governing bodies, the NHS and the law.

Invalid information can come from sources such as social media and the press and can often be referred to as 'fake news'. However, it should be noted that social media and the press can contain some valid information.

obtaining information from more than one source

If information is obtained from more than one source, its validity is more likely to be authenticated, by cross-checking the information from one source to another.

sources of information example

Beryl has read an article in a newspaper that states that the standard rate of VAT is 20%. Beryl checked the validity of this information by looking at the VAT pages of the gov.uk website, therefore confirming that the information was correct.

The benefits of obtaining information from more than one source are:

- to confirm the accuracy of the information

- to check that the information is up to date

- to act as reassurance that this information can be passed to other users of the information as a reliable source

PRIMARY AND SECONDARY SOURCES OF INFORMATION

Information can be classed as:

- primary – which is original and has not been altered

- secondary – an interpretation of a primary source of information

Examples of primary and secondary sources of information are shown in the following table.

primary sources	secondary sources
■ novels ■ audio and video recordings ■ emails ■ interviews ■ letters ■ official documents ■ photographs ■ paintings ■ legal text	■ textbooks ■ dictionaries ■ biographies ■ magazine and newspaper articles ■ documentaries ■ reviews ■ essays

primary and secondary sources general example

A primary source could be a photograph of an event that has happened, such as a wedding.

A secondary source could be a documentary about the wedding.

primary and secondary sources business example

A primary source could be the budget which is presented by the UK government each year.

A secondary source could be a webinar explaining the implications of the budget to businesses.

INFORMATION AND THE FINANCE FUNCTION

choosing information

When completing tasks in a finance environment, it is important to understand that a variety of information may be available. Therefore selecting the correct information is essential to the completion of a task competently.

the bank statement

The bank statement, illustrated below, is probably the most common document that finance staff will need to deal with. It is a record of the financial transactions that pass through the bank account; it may be a hard copy, downloaded from the bank or connected to the accounting software via bank feeds.

United Bank plc
The Square, Broadfield, BR9 2AS

Account title	Trends
Account number	20963513
Statement	49

Date	Details	Payments (debits)	Receipts (credits)	Balance
20-3				
3 Nov	Balance brought down			1,678.90 CR
10 Nov	BASCS Peony Fashions 27641 ▨		1,427.85	3,106.75 CR
10 Nov	238628 ▨	249.57		2,857.18 CR
11 Nov	238629 ▨	50.00		2,807.18 CR
13 Nov	Cardline receipts ▨		267.45	3,074.63 CR
17 Nov	Transfer (Deposit A/C) ▨		400.00	3,474.63 CR
21 Nov	238630 ▨	783.90		2,690.73 CR
24 Nov	238626 ▨	127.00		2,563.73 CR
24 Nov	Albionet Websales 209635513 ▨		1,169.00	3,732.73 CR
25 Nov	DD Westmid Power ▨	589.30		3,143.43 CR
28 Nov	Bank Charges ▨	87.50		3,055.93 CR

It is important that employees working in the finance function can identify items on a bank statement. Situations where this is required include:

- checking entries in the cash book of the business against the bank statement (a 'bank reconciliation statement')

- answering a query from a customer or a colleague to see if the business has received an electronic bank transfer payment the customer has made

Some of the common bank account entries (in the Details column) are listed below. The numbers shown here have been added for easy reference.

■ **cheques** – the entry in the Details column will be a number, for example, '238628'

■ **electronic bank transfers received** – the entry in the Details column may contain the full details, for example: 'BACS Peony Fashions 27641'

■ **credit or debit cards payments received** – see the entries in the Details column 'Cardline receipts' and also 'Albionet Websales 209635513'

■ **internal bank transfers** – for example, a transfer from a deposit account to the current account of the business – see the entry 'Transfer (Deposit A/C)'

■ **direct debit payments out** – for example, paying bills or insurance premiums – see the entry 'DD Westmid Power'

■ **bank charges** – the charge made by the bank for running the account; this might be made monthly or quarterly

information required for bookkeeping

Bookkeepers will often use the bank statement as their primary source.

Information must relate to the correct business and be for the correct business.

Supporting documentation, such as sales invoices, purchases invoices and receipts must be checked for their authenticity.

information required for preparing a budget

In order to compile a budget (a financial forecast), a business will require several sources of information, which may include:

■ a list of customers, orders and prices

■ a list of suppliers, products and prices

■ details of employees and their pay rates

■ details of current contracts for rent, gas, electricity and phones

■ details of any major planned expenditure and maintenance

■ the financial statements from the previous year

The example that follows is an extract from the financial statements for Anne Field Fashions for the previous year, which can be used as a basis for preparation of the budget.

STATEMENT OF PROFIT OR LOSS: ANNE FIELD FASHIONS
for the year ended 30 JUNE 20-7

	£000	£000
Sales revenue		85,500
Opening inventory	13,250	
Purchases	55,000	
	68,250	
Less Closing inventory	18,100	
Cost of sales		50,150
Gross Profit		35,350
Less expenses:		
Administration expenses	1,180	
Wages	9,220	
Rent paid	1,200	
Telephone	800	
		12,400
Profit for the year		22,950

providing information

The finance function provides information to others, both internally and externally.

Examples of information provided by the finance function are shown in the following table.

in practice	in a finance department
▪ bookkeeping	▪ sales reports
▪ VAT returns	▪ purchases and expenditure reports
▪ payroll	▪ budgets
▪ tax returns	▪ inventory records
▪ financial statements	▪ monthly accounts

It is important that this information is useful to the end user; therefore, **useful information** has the following **characteristics**:

▪ **comparable** – the information should be easily compared with similar information

for example, comparing the performance of one department with another

- **consistent** – the information should be prepared with a consistent approach

  for example, applying the same accounting methods, such as how inventory is valued in different accounting periods

- **understandable** – the information should be clear and easy to use

  for example, showing the performance of a sales department graphically, with supporting terminology that is understood by the sales team

- **relevant and reliable** – the information should be relevant to the task required and obtained from a reliable source

  for example, a report of the cash flow of a business will use information from the most recent bank statements

- **timely** – the information should be provided within sufficient time for decisions to be made

  for example, reporting the month end accounts within a reasonable period of time, such as by the end of the following month

- **accurate** – the information should be sufficiently accurate to be relied upon

  for example, confirming the accuracy of figures within reports, by carrying out reconciliations and producing control accounts

- **complete** – information should contain everything that is required, but should not be too excessive

  for example, an individual member of the sales team may need to see a complete list of all sales made, whereas a sales manager may just need to see a report on the totals from each member of the sales team

the importance of providing useful information

The completion of a VAT return is an example of how important it is that information provided by the finance function is complete, accurate and submitted to HMRC on time.

If any of these qualities is missing, the VAT return will be defective and this could cause a lot of problems for a business. HMRC can demand penalties in serious cases where VAT returns are:

- incomplete – for example, missing important data because of an accounting error such as excluding significant amounts of VAT on sales

- inaccurate – for example, incorrect data resulting from an arithmetic error within the accounting system

- late – not submitted within the required deadline

It is the role of staff in the finance function to be efficient and work to a high standard in providing the required information.

DOCUMENTS RECEIVED BY FINANCE

The finance function of a business, whether large or small, will receive lots of information and documents in different formats.

documents received from a customer

The type of documents that a business may receive from a customer include:

- purchase orders – giving details of goods or services ordered
- remittance advice – giving details of the amounts paid to the business

The finance staff must have a good working knowledge of both documents in order to:

- check the details of the written contents
- check any figures

They will look for possible mistakes including:

- if the product code or goods description on a purchase order are not read properly by the seller the wrong goods could be sent out
- if a mistake in the amount sent is not detected on a remittance advice the wrong amount will be paid

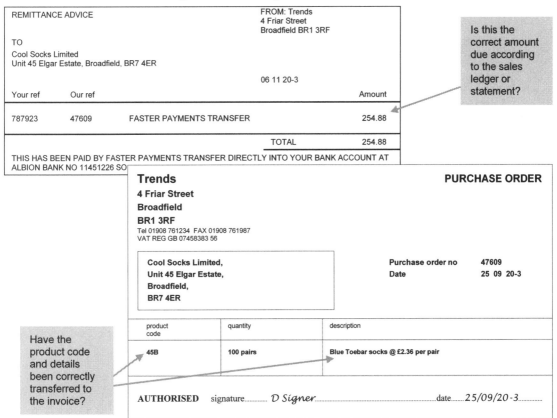

documents received from a supplier

The key documents which may be received from a supplier include:

- supplier invoices – giving details of goods and services bought by the business

- supplier credit notes – giving details of goods and services returned by the business

- statements of account – showing the amount that the business owes to the supplier

This is a key document which needs to be checked very carefully by the finance staff. The items to check – as shown below – will be:

- the balance brought forward from an earlier period

- payments made (for example, Faster Payment bank transfer)

- invoices and credit notes received

If these are all correct, payment should be made according to the terms granted by the seller.

other documents received

The finance function staff will also have to deal with information and documents received from other external stakeholders, in paper format or electronic formats. These might include bank statements and credit card statements for business credit cards.

Documents which may be received from other parts of a business include budgetary information, inventory records and costing information.

FINANCIAL INFORMATION PRODUCED

the day-to-day finance function

The finance function will provide documents externally on a daily basis, including:

to customers	to suppliers
▪ sales invoices	▪ purchase orders
▪ delivery notes	▪ remittance advices
▪ credit notes	
▪ statements of account	

financial information for decision making

One of the functions of the staff working in the finance function is to provide information to management so that they can monitor the financial performance of the business. The managers will then be able to make informed financial decisions about the running of the business. Examples of these types of information and the ways in which they help decision making are:

▪ sales reports

▪ unit cost reports

▪ budget reports

sales reports

It is important that the management of a business is always made aware of the level of sales made for a range of products on at least a monthly basis. This is critical because the level of sales achieved will affect the level of profit made.

A **sales report** will enable the finance function and the sales and marketing departments to see exactly what products are doing well and which are not selling. As a result of this analysis the following decisions and recommendations could be made, depending on the circumstances:

- a **fall** in sales of Product A: increase marketing; scale down production

- an **increase** in sales of Product A: consider increasing its price (depending on the competition); increase production to meet demand

Sales reports are often set up on a spreadsheet which is updated monthly. The spreadsheet below might contain the following types of data:

- **actual** monthly sales figures per product or type of product set out in separate columns for each month

- total **cumulative** sales figures by product set out in a separate column

◇	A	B	C	D	E	F	G
1			Monthly sales report (£) 20-7				
2		January	February	March	April	May	Cumulative total
3	Product A	1,423	985	963	655	728	4,754
4	Product B	1,609	1,096	1,066	715	815	5,301
5	Product C	8,525	5,438	5,025	3,048	4,169.1	26,205
6	Product D	7,444.42	5,096.05	4,951.36	3,215.71	3,709.93	24,417
7	Product E	593.21	419.06	398.35	270.38	310.82	1,992
8	TOTAL SALES	19,594.63	13,034.11	12,403.71	7,904.09	9,732.85	62,669

unit cost reports

One of the roles of the finance function is to break down the total cost of producing a product into various different costs:

- materials used (a variable cost)

- the cost of labour (a variable cost)

- fixed costs (for example, insurance and heating)

This information is used by the finance function to work out the total cost of producing different quantities of that product. Management can then make the decision as to how many units to produce at a time at the lowest cost per item (unit cost). It must however make sure that it can sell that number of items. For example, if a stationery business prints diaries every year, there is no point in printing a very large number on the grounds that they will cost less because at the end of the year they go out of date.

In the example below, if 1,000 units of an item cost £13 each to make and 1,500 units cost £11 each, the business is more likely to make 1,500 units, as long as it is confident of selling them.

Comparative unit costing for 1,000 and 1,500 units (£)				
	A	B	C	D	E
1		1,000 units		1,500 units	
2		**Total Cost**	**Unit Cost**	**Total Cost**	**Unit Cost**
3	Materials	£6,000	£6	£7,500	£5
4	Labour	£2,000	£2	£3,000	£2
5	Fixed costs	£5,000	£5	£6,000	£4
6	Total	£13,000	£13	£16,500	£11

budget reports

Another role of the finance function is to plan ahead and create budgets.

A budget is a financial plan for a future period of time which estimates the likely income and costs for products made or services provided.

Budgets are useful for monitoring financial performance, answering questions like 'how well are sales performing?' or 'are our costs being kept within the planned limit?'

A critical part of the budgeting process is comparing actual performance, for example sales achieved, against the planned 'budgeted' sales. The numerical difference between the budgeted sales and the actual sales is known as a variance. A variance can be:

■ a **favourable** (FAV) variance (a good result); this happens when

– sales are higher than budgeted

– costs are lower than budgeted

■ an **adverse** (ADV) variance (a poor result); this happens when

– sales are lower than budgeted

– costs are higher than budgeted

An example of a cost budget (set up as a spreadsheet) is shown on the following page.

	A	B	C	D	E
1		Budget £	Actual £	Variance £	Adv/Fav
2	Direct materials	60,000	64,000	4,000	Adv
3	Direct labours	24,000	25,000	1,000	Adv
4	Overheads	12,000	10,000	2,000	Fav
5	Totals	96,000	99,000	3,000	Adv

Note that:

■ there are two adverse (adv) variances – direct materials were £4,000 more than budgeted and direct labour was £1,000 more than budgeted – so the business is a total of £5,000 over target

■ there is only one favourable (fav) variance – this is where the actual overhead costs of £10,000 were £2,000 less than the budgeted £12,000

■ the total of budgeted and actual costs are totalled to produce a net adverse (ADV) variance of £3,000

the importance of budget reports in the finance function

The importance of a budget is that it is a very useful planning tool. Managers in the finance function need to know what their **targets** are. Managers also need to **monitor** progress and so it is important that the finance staff provide them with accurate and up-to-date figures. If the performance of the business is not on target – and particularly when it is below target – the managers can then take control of the situation by carrying out actions to rectify the situation.

CASH AND TAX INFORMATION

The documents and information which are produced to monitor cash and calculate taxes may be produced internally by the finance department, or produced externally by accountants, depending on the size and nature of the business.

cash

The management of a business will want to monitor its cash position. 'Cash' in this sense includes physical cash held in the business and bank account balances. We saw in Chapter 4 the importance of maintaining the **solvency** of a business, ie ensuring that the business is able to pay its debts when they are due. There are a number of sources of information which are useful in providing this information:

■ regular **bank statements**

■ an up-to-date **cash budget**

tax on profits

Any UK business, whether sole trader, partnership or limited company, will have to pay tax on its profits.

The sources of information which are used to show any tax due are:

- the financial statements of the business, showing the profit
- tax computations, which add back items that are not allowable for tax purposes
- annual tax returns
- statements received from HMRC

tax on sales

Any UK business that sells goods or services over a certain limit will need to register for **VAT** and add VAT to sales. The VAT due is paid to HMRC, after deducting any allowable VAT on purchases and expenses.

The sources of information which are used to show any VAT due are:

- sales invoices and credit notes issued
- purchase invoices and credit notes received
- expenditure paid
- VAT returns

INFORMATION AND DIGITAL TECHNOLOGY

the link between data and information

Data is unprocessed facts and figures.

Data is processed and transformed into **information**; the information will allow decisions to be made.

The stages of converting data into information includes:

- the collection of raw data from internal and external sources
- processing the data through analysis and the removal of non-relevant data
- interpreting the data by adding value and transforming it to information
- reporting on the information by disseminating (making it available) to the required user

For example, raw data could be a list of prices. By applying the list of prices to products, a consumer can make the decision about whether or not to buy a certain product.

digital technology

Most businesses exist with some, if not complete, reliance on digital technologies.

The use of technology vastly improves the speed by which raw data can be processed. However, the value of the information that can be provided to any business by the use of technology must be compared to its cost.

The benefits of using digital technology include:

- the use of automatic bank feeds
- automatic uploads of receipts and invoices from scans or photos
- sending invoices and statements to customers via email
- data is usually only entered once; in a manual system the same data may be entered several times
- errors are minimised
- time is saved
- some processes, such as reconciliations, are carried out automatically. However, they will still need to be checked for completeness and accuracy (therefore staff will need appropriate training which will add to the cost)

THE IMPORTANCE OF DATA AND INFORMATION SECURITY

types of data and information

Data and information can be numerical or in the form of text and is normally held in two main formats: paper-based and computer-based. The finance function could be dealing with:

- **paper-based data** such as:
  - financial documents generated internally
  - financial documents received from customers and suppliers
  - printouts of spreadsheets
  - internal policies and procedures
  - letters
- **computer-based data** such as:
  - computer-based accounting
  - spreadsheets used for sales reports and budgeting
  - payroll
  - emails

the need for security and confidentiality

Finance staff always have to take care with confidentiality of information held both in paper records and also on computers. For example:

- payroll information should always be kept strictly confidential and not revealed to other employees
- information about customers and suppliers should never be revealed to people outside of the organisation

The **Data Protection Act 2018** is an important piece of legislation which protects the confidentiality of information about individuals. It applies to:

- personal data about identifiable individuals (for example sole traders and partners), but not about companies
- records held electronically, for example a computer database of names, addresses, telephone numbers, sales details of each customer (the data subject)
- manual records – for example, a card index file system of customer details

All organisations which process personal data must register with the Information Commissioner's office (ICO) and should follow the key principles set out under the General Data Protection Regulation (GDPR). These principles require that personal data is handled properly and there must be a valid lawful basis for processing personal data.

The key principles under GDPR are:

1 lawfulness, fairness and transparency
processed lawfully, fairly and in a transparent manner in relation to individuals

2 purpose limitation
collected for specified, explicit and legitimate purposes and not further processed in a manner that is incompatible with those purposes; further processing for archiving purposes in the public interest, scientific or historical research purposes or statistical purposes shall not be considered to be incompatible with the initial purposes

3 data minimisation
adequate, relevant and limited to what is necessary in relation to the purposes for which they are processed

4 accuracy
accurate and, where necessary, kept up to date; every reasonable step must be taken to ensure that personal data that are inaccurate, having regard to the purposes for which they are processed, are erased or rectified without delay

5 storage limitation

kept in a form which permits identification of data subjects for no longer than is necessary for the purposes for which the personal data are processed; personal data may be stored for longer periods insofar as the personal data will be processed solely for archiving purposes in the public interest, scientific or historical research purposes or statistical purposes subject to implementation of the appropriate technical and organisational measures required by the GDPR in order to safeguard the rights and freedoms of individuals

6 integrity and confidentiality

processed in a manner that ensures appropriate security of the personal data, including protection against unauthorised or unlawful processing and against accidental loss, destruction or damage, using appropriate technical or organisational measures

7 accountability

to take responsibility for what is done with personal data and how the other principles are complied with, appropriate measures and records must be in place to be able to demonstrate compliance

Individuals have the legal right to know what personal details about them are held by an organisation and can apply to the organisation for a copy of the personal data held.

You will not need to be able to quote this Act, but you should know that it states that personal data must be accurate, kept only as long as necessary and kept securely. It requires that an organisation should not reveal, without permission, personal information about its customers to other customers or any information about its employees.

DATA AND INFORMATION STORAGE AND ACCESS

paper-based data – filing and archiving

Paper-based data, including financial documents and letters, are normally initially stored in individual files kept in filing cabinets so that they can be easily accessed. After a period of time the business will need to 'archive' them, ie store them in safe place which can be accessed if they are needed. Traditionally records of this nature are kept for six years plus the current year. Sensitive data such as staff records will need to be locked and the keys only made available to senior staff.

computer-based data

Nowadays the large majority of information is processed and stored digitally. Because of the ease in which computer data can be accessed, copied and transmitted, great care must be taken to control:

■ the access by staff to data

■ the safe storage of data

■ the protection of data against intrusion from the outside by hackers and viruses

Computer-based data will therefore require:

■ the use of passwords

■ secure and multiple back-ups

■ virus protection software

We will deal with each of these in turn.

software passwords – accessing a program

Passwords are also needed to protect sensitive and confidential data held on the computer system. This is particularly important in the areas of staff records and also in the case of financial data processed by computer accounting programs.

One solution to the problem of unauthorised employees gaining access to sensitive financial data is the use of **passwords** to gain access to a computer program. Many software packages require users to access data by completing a two-step verification process before access is permitted.

Many larger businesses will employ a number of people who need to operate the computer accounting system; they will be issued with an appropriate password. Businesses can also set up **access rights** which restrict certain employees to certain activities and prevent them from accessing more sensitive areas such as the making of payments from the bank account.

the need for strong passwords

A safe password is known as a 'strong' password. There is no use in creating a password which is easily worked out, for example 'password' (it does happen), the name and date of birth of your partner, your favourite football team or pet rabbit. Passwords must ideally:

■ be at least eight characters long

■ not contain your username, real name, or company name

■ not contain a complete word.

■ be significantly different from previous passwords

The password must ideally contain characters from each of the following four categories:

- uppercase letters, for example, A, B, C
- lowercase letters, for example, a, b, c
- numbers, for example, 0, 1, 2, 3, 4, 5, 6, 7, 8, 9
- keyboard symbols, for example, @ % & * _ ? /

Also it goes without saying that you should not leave your password where it is accessible, for example, on a post-it note on your computer, in the front of your diary or in your phone.

backing-up files

You will also need to **back-up** the data generated by the computer. There is no set rule about when you should do this, but it should be at least at the end of every day and preferably when you have completed a long run of inputting.

back-up processes

If you are working on a network, you can normally save your files to your workstation's hard disk and also to the server. If you have a standalone computer system, the back-up files should be saved to some form of storage device. This may take the form of:

- a hard drive in the workstation itself
- an external portable hard drive kept securely in the office
- an external portable hard drive taken off the premises

Another back-up option is to back up files on a server at a remote location or direct to the 'cloud'.

It is important that an organisation works out a systematic policy for back-up of its data. This could involve:

- daily back-ups held both on and off the premises
- a 'time machine' hard drive which records and stores files at regular short intervals – in other words it will enable you to go 'back in time' to recover files at an earlier stage of production if a file becomes corrupted or accidentally deleted

anti-virus software

Anti-virus software is a 'must' for any organisation such as a business which uses the internet. This software, also known as **anti-malware** software, is computer software which is used to set up an effective shield against intrusive and destructive **malware** which can wipe your files, disable your software and then spread via the internet to other computer users. Malware should be kept at bay at all costs.

cyber security

Cyber security is how individuals and organisations reduce the risk of cyber-attacks.

The function of cyber security is to protect the **devices** we all use (smartphones, laptops, tablets and computers), and the **services** we access - both online and at work - from theft or damage by using firewall software.

It's also about preventing unauthorised access to the vast amounts of **personal information** we store on these devices, and online. Phishing is when someone pretends to be someone from an organisation and is an attack to steal data.

Cyber security is important because smartphones, computers and the internet are now such a fundamental part of modern life, that it's difficult to imagine how we'd function without them. From online banking and shopping, to email and social media, it's more important than ever to take steps that can prevent cyber criminals getting hold of our accounts, data, and devices.

Cyber attacks can be avoided by taking steps such as checking the authenticity of emails received, not clicking on unauthorised links on files and avoiding downloading information from unsafe websites. Users should take steps to ensure that when sensitive information is requested from websites, the website is legitimate and if the user is unsure, carry out further checks, such as phoning the organisation or seeking advice from the IT department.

Chapter Summary

■ Information can be obtained from a huge variety of sources; therefore, it is important to check its validity.

■ Information can be from primary and secondary sources.

■ People working in a finance function must be familiar with the range of information and documents they deal with on a day-to-day basis.

■ Documents are likely to be received from external sources such as customers, suppliers and the banks, for example invoices, credit notes and bank statements.

■ Information and documents are produced within the finance function for use by other areas of the business and also by the management of the finance function, for example sales figures, cash budgets and financial statements.

■ Information and documents will also be produced by the finance function for sending out to external stakeholders. for example sales and purchases documentation, financial statements showing profit or loss and details of financing, and returns to HMRC.

■ The importance of the characteristices of useful information must be understood. Information should be comparable, consistent, understandable, relevant and reliable, timely, accurate and complete.

■ It is very important that any information produced or stored by the finance function, whether on paper or electronically, is kept securely. Finance employees must use suitable safe computer passwords where required, back-up data regularly, ensure suitable anti-virus software is installed and be aware of the threat of cyber security.

Key Terms	**information**	the knowledge gained from investigation, study or instruction
	primary sources of information	original information which has not been altered
	secondary sources of information	an interpretation of a primary source of information
	budget	a financial plan produced by the finance function for a future period of time; it estimates the likely income and costs of products made or services provided
	sales report	a schedule produced by the finance function showing sales by product or product range by month, set up as a report for management, often on a spreadsheet
	unit cost report	a report produced by the finance function which breaks down for management the total cost of producing a product into material, labour and fixed costs
	cash budget	a forecast produced by the finance function showing the receipts and payments of money through the bank account of a business and the way in which they affect the bank balance each month
	data	unprocessed facts and figures
	data security	the need to keep personal data held by a business securely and confidentially
	Data Protection Act	the law which sets out how personal data held by a business should be held securely and confidentially
	archiving	the process of storing data securely over a period of time so that it can be easily accessed
	passwords	a unique mixture of characters (ie letters, numbers and symbols) which can give access by employees to computer systems; used for keeping data safe and confidential
	cyber security	protecting devices used and services accessed online

Activities

5.1 Identify whether the following are primary or secondary sources of information:

		Primary	Secondary
(a)	A certificate of incorporation for a company		
(b)	A tutorial book about personal tax		
(c)	An Act of Parliament		

5.2 A business always uses the First in First Out (FIFO) method for inventory valuation. This is an example of:

(a)	understandable information	
(b)	accurate information	
(c)	consistent information	
(d)	timely information	

Tick the **one** correct option.

5.3 It is important to check a remittance advice when it is received because:

(a)	There might be an error with a product code quoted, resulting in the wrong goods being supplied	
(b)	The total may not agree with the total on the statement of account sent by the seller	
(c)	The wrong VAT rate may have been applied on the invoice sent	

Tick the **one** correct option.

5.4   It is important for a seller to check a purchase order for goods when it is received because:

(a)	The product code may not agree with the description of the goods and so it will need to be queried	
(b)	The total may not agree with the total on the statement of account sent by the seller	
(c)	It does not include a VAT calculation	

Tick the **one** correct option.

5.5   It is important for a business that has bought goods to check a statement of account issued by the seller because:

(a)	The VAT amounts will need to be recorded in the accounting system	
(b)	The amounts sent by the buyer in settlement of invoices must be correctly shown on the statement	
(c)	It might include bank charges which will need looking into	

Tick the **one** correct option.

5.6   Complete the two sentences below using the following phrases:

sales are higher than budgeted	**sales are lower than budgeted**
costs are lower than budgeted	**costs are higher than budgeted**

A favourable variance occurs when |_____|

or |_____| .

An adverse variance occurs when |_____|

or |_____| .

5.7   A business is most likely to be able to manage its cash position effectively by:

(a)	Filing its bank statements safely and confidentially	
(b)	Maximising the number of payments made by electronic transfer	
(c)	Preparing a cash budget	

Tick the **one** correct option.

5.8   A business will be able to calculate the amount of tax it has to pay by preparing:

(a)	A unit cost report	
(b)	A statement of profit or loss	

Tick the **one** correct option.

5.9   Keeping confidentiality within a business means:

(a)	Keeping data backed up in more than one format	
(b)	Being truthful and honest in your dealings	
(c)	Not releasing personal data to outsiders	

Tick the **one** correct option.

5.10   Creating passwords for accessing software requires that the password must be 'strong' and not easily broken (guessed). List the following four passwords in order of strength (ie the strongest password first).

mypassword   **pass2A%**   **kith33**   **G5Thrones**

1	
2	
3	
4	

5.11 Backing up of computer data within a business should ideally be carried out:

(a)	At least daily	
(b)	In more than one storage format	
(c)	Stored only on the premises	
(d)	Only stored externally	
(e)	Stored on the premises and also externally	

Tick **all** the correct options.

6 Business communications

this chapter covers...

This chapter explains the need for people working in the finance function to be able to communicate with work colleagues and also with people outside the workplace – customers and suppliers, for example.

- *Effective communication needs to be:*
  - *clear, structured and presented logically*
  - *appropriate to the situation and easily understood*
  - *accurate and technically correct*
- *Communication may be:*
  - *internal within the business or external, eg with customers and suppliers*
  - *verbal or written*
  - *presented on paper or processed on a computer*
- *The specific types of communication covered in this chapter include:*
  - *business letters*
  - *emails*
  - *social media*
  - *notes*
  - *business reports*
  - *spreadsheets*
- *The language used in business communications is generally more formal than everyday language used with friends and family*
- *Inappropriate communication will have consequences for both businesses and the individual*

THE NEED TO COMMUNICATE

the need for effective communication

If you are communicating a message to another person or group of people, that message must be **effective** to be successful. In Chapter 4 we established that effective communication should be:

- clear and easily understood

- concise – not too long-winded

- unambiguous, using straightforward language so that the meaning cannot be misinterpreted

- complete – the whole message must be there

- accurate – there is no point in unintentionally misleading people

- provided at the right time – not too early and not too late (timely)

- appropriate to the person or people receiving it and to meet their needs

- in the most appropriate format (medium), whether by phone, message, email, letter or report

forms of communication – the methods used

There are many methods of communication that can be used. Recently, methods of communication have evolved, especially with the restrictions imposed by Covid19.

There is normally a clear choice for most circumstances, although occasionally it can be effective if a normally accepted method is changed if the circumstances demand it. For example, a telephone call may be more effective than yet another unanswered email in dealing with a potential problem, communication being better than silence.

The choice of communication methods used involve a number of classifications:

- **verbal** or **written** methods of communication:

    - verbal: telephone calls, voicemail messages, in-house meetings, conference calls using technology such as Teams and Zoom

    - written: business letters, reports, notes

- written communication can be **paper-based** or **electronic**:

    - paper-based: letters, notes, reports

    - electronic: emails, texts, messaging, intranet and social media

The choice will normally be based on custom, ie 'what is normally done'. The variety of possible methods is shown in the diagram set out below.

In the rest of the chapter we will describe some of the more common communication methods – including business letters, emails, notes for verbal messages, business reports and spreadsheets.

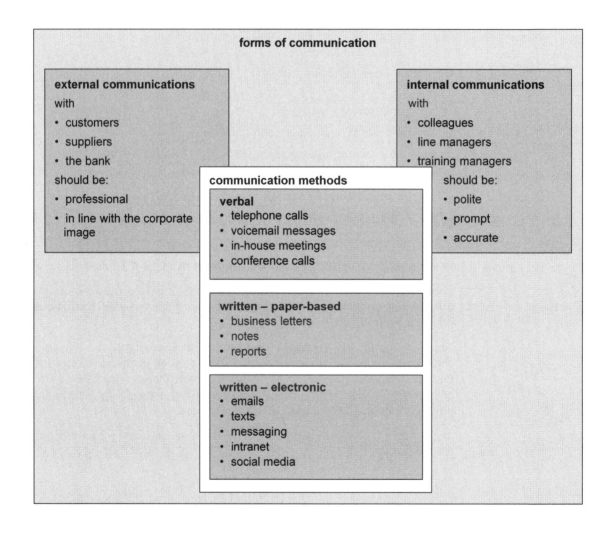

BUSINESS LETTERS

When you deal with business letters you will see that the appearance and format of each letter is in a uniform 'house' style, a style which identifies that business, and is common to all letters that it sends. The letter will normally be on standard printed stationery showing the name, address and details of the business, and will be set out with headings, paragraphs, signatures – the 'elements' of the letter – in a uniform way.

There are a number of different ways of setting out the text of a letter. The most common of these used in business is illustrated and explained on the next two pages.

characteristics of a business letter

The most commonly-used letter format is known as a 'fully blocked' style:

- all the lines start at the left margin

- the use of open punctuation, ie there is no punctuation, except in the main body of the letter, which uses normal punctuation

- paragraphs are divided by a space, and are not indented

- a fully blocked letter is easy to key in as all the lines are set uniformly to the left margin

elements of the letter

The explanations which follow refer to the letter shown on page 125.

printed letterhead The name and address of the business is normally printed on the paper and must be up-to-date.

reference The reference on the letter illustrated (DH/SB/69) is a standard format:
- DH (Derek Hunt), the writer
- SB (Sally Burgess), the secretary
- 69, the number of the file where the correspondence is kept

If you need to quote the reference of a letter to which you are replying, the references will be quoted as follows: Your ref TR/FG/45 Our ref DH/SB/69.

date	The date is entered in date (number), month (word), year (number) order.
recipient	The name and address of the person to whom the letter is sent. This section of the letter may be displayed in the window of a window envelope, so it is essential that it is accurate.
salutation	'Dear Sir. . . Dear Madam' – if you know the person's name and title (ie Mr, Mrs, Miss, Ms) use it, but check that it is correct – a misspelt name or an incorrect title will ruin an otherwise competent letter.
heading	The heading sets out the subject matter of the letter – it will concentrate the reader's mind.
body	The body of the letter is an area where the message of the letter is set out. The text must:
	– be laid out in short precise paragraphs and short clear sentences
	– start with a point of reference (eg referring to an invoice)
	– set out the message in a logical sequence
	– be written in plain English – but avoid 'slang' expressions and, equally, avoid unusual or old-fashioned words which obscure the meaning
	– finish with a clear indication of the next step to be taken (eg please telephone, please arrange an appointment, please buy our products, please pay our invoice)
complimentary close	The complimentary close (signing off phrase) must be consistent with the salutation:
	'Dear Sir/Dear Madam' followed by 'Yours faithfully'
	'Dear Mr Sutton/Dear Ms Jones' followed by 'Yours sincerely'.
name and job title	It is essential for the reader to know the name of the person who sent the letter, and that person's job title, because a reply will need to be addressed to a specific person.
enclosures	If there are enclosures with the letter such as a copy invoice or statement, the abbreviation 'enc' or 'encl' is used at the bottom of the letter.

the 'house style' letter

Wyvern Motor Supplies
107 High Street
Mereford
MR1 9SZ
Tel 01605 675365   Fax 01605 765576   Email sales@WMSupplies.co.uk

reference ——→ Ref DH/SB/69

date ——→ 15 December 20-7

name and address
of recipient ——→ Purchasing Department
Osborne Car Accessories
17 Pump Street
Mereford MR6
7ER

salutation ——→ Dear Sir

heading ——→ Invoice 8288 £10,589.50

body of
the letter ——→ We note from our records that we have not yet received
payment of our invoice 8288 dated 15 September 20-7.
Our up-to-date statement of account is enclosed,
together with a copy of the invoice.
Our payment terms are strictly 30 days from the date
of the invoice. We shall be grateful if you will
settle the £10,589.50 without further delay.
We look forward to receiving your payment.

complimentary
close ——→ Yours faithfully

signature ——→ *D M Hunt*

name and job title ——→ Derek Hunt Accounts Manager

enclosures ——→ enc

EMAILS

'netiquette' – the art of email writing

There is an accepted set of rules of 'what to do' and 'what not to do' when writing a business email; this is sometimes referred to as 'netiquette.' If you work for an organisation you must ensure that you are familiar with the ways in which emails are written and dealt with. It is essential that you always project a professional image of your organisation when composing and replying to an email.

Although professional emails are seen as being more informal than letters, there is no excuse for careless mistakes, use of texting language, emoticons (eg smileys), LOTS OF CAPITAL LETTERS and exclamation marks!!!!!!!

Study the email shown below and then read the hints that follow.

recipient

It is obviously important to get the email address right.

subject

Keep the subject description short and to the point. Use a capital letter for the start of the first word.

Cc

The 'Cc' (carbon copy) is used to send a message to a group of people, and each person in the group who receives the message will see the addresses of the others in the list. These people should therefore ideally know each other. 'Cc' should only be used if you are happy that they are all aware that the others on the list are receiving the message. If it is used to send a message to a group of strangers you may annoy them and breach privacy regulations.

Bcc

'Bcc' (blind carbon copy) is an option (not shown on the illustration) which can be used to email a group of contacts who do not know each other. 'Bcc' allows the message to go to a group, but the group members do not know that it is a group mailing as they do not see the details of the other recipients.

addressing the recipient

How do you address your new contacts? It all depends on the relationship. If the person is well known to you, the usual 'Hi Ramjit,' 'Hello Laura,' is quite acceptable. The approach is very similar to a telephone call. If you do not know the recipient you should be very formal: 'Dear Mr Lubowski,' 'Dear Ms. Terry,' and so on. You should remain on formal terms until in due course it is clear from the other person that you can say 'Hi Sue,' or whatever is required.

signing off

On the whole you should use the same process as you would if you were writing a business letter. If you start with 'Dear Mr Brown' you should finish with 'Yours sincerely' although there is a tendency now also to use 'kind regards' or 'best wishes' instead.

how formal should the text be?

An email is different from a letter in this respect. The level of formality will depend on the relationship with the recipient. Whatever the level of formality, an email should have correct spelling, grammar and punctuation. Ideally, sentences should be short and separated into distinct paragraphs.

It makes the message clearer if you put a blank line between paragraphs.

If it is an **internal** email, a degree of informality is more normal – eg 'Hi Jon,' 'Regards, Mike' and so on. In practice close colleagues will sometimes abbreviate even further – eg 'John, the Huxborough contract needs signing. Thanks. Geoff.'

some email do's and do nots

Do . . .

■ keep the message short and to the point

■ when replying, answer the points raised in the incoming message and reply or confirm receipt of the message on the same day

■ read through and edit what you have written before you send it

■ make sure the original message 'thread' is included when replying

Do not . . .

■ use text in CAPITAL LETTERS - THIS IS KNOWN AS 'SHOUTING'

■ use too much formatting, eg underlines, different fonts, bright colours

■ send large attachments which might clog up the recipient's email system

■ say something in an email that you would not say to someone's face

INTRANET

The **intranet** is a computer network for sharing information and accessing and sharing files, which allows secure communication, back up and data security within an organisation, usually excluding anybody that is external to the organisation.

SOCIAL MEDIA

Social media consists of websites and applications that enable the users of technology to create and share content and to participate in social networking.

The most significant benefits in the use of social media are the increase in the speed of communication and the audience that can be reached through its use.

Social media includes:

■ social networks – a social media site which allows individuals to connect with family and friends

■ bookmarking sites – users can save and organise links to online resources and websites

■ social news – users can post news links and links to other external articles

■ media sharing – users can share different types of media, such as images and videos

- microblogging – users can submit short written entries
- forums – users can engage in conversations by posting and responding to community messages
- social review sites – reviews about products and services

NOTES

notes to others

A traditional form of communication within an organisation is the written **note**. This can be:

- an informal written note, passing on a message or an instruction
- a telephone message you pass on to a colleague (some organisations use pre-printed telephone message pads)

The important elements of a written note are:

- the name of the person who is sending the note
- the name of the person who is to receive the note
- the time and date that the note is written
- a clearly stated message
- a clear indication of any action to be taken as a result of the message

The examples of notes that follow contain all these elements.

To Tim Blackstock,
Order Processing

Please remember to allow PDT Ltd an extra 10% trade discount on invoices this month.

John Tregennick, Sales
3.04.-7   10.30

TELEPHONE MESSAGES

TO   Karin Schmidt. Accounts
FROM   H Khan, Sales
DATE   22 April 20-7
TIME   12.30

Please ring Jim Stoat at RF Electronics – he is complaining that they have not received a credit note for returned damaged inventory (order ref 823423). Please treat urgently – he is not happy!

HK

Nowadays, **the intranet** is a more common method for passing on messages and making requests electronically within an organisation.

the importance of effective note taking

It is common practice in everyday life to summarise in note form 'things that have to be done', for example compiling a shopping list or a list of jobs for the weekend. The memory is not always totally reliable in this respect.

There are instances at work where you may have to do the same sort of thing, for example a daily 'to do' list.

It may also be possible that you have to prepare for some form of **verbal communication** that is required, for example:

■ a 'report back' to an internal meeting of a subject you have been asked to look into, eg the levels of discount given by your competitors

■ an explanation of a new office procedure to other staff

■ a list of topics to bring up at a staff appraisal, eg performance, promotion and pay

■ an important phone call to a customer about a complex technical issue

■ to prepare for a meeting with other team members

■ to ensure you remember what is required from a one to one meeting with a manager

In each case, each item on the list you compile should ideally be:

■ clear, short and to the point, not too wordy

■ preceded by numbers or bullet points

■ set out in a logical order

Again, remember the other key relevant points from effective communication in your note taking. Notes should be:

■ easily understood

■ unambiguous

■ complete

■ accurate

REPORTS

written reports

A written report is a way of informing a person or a group of people about a specific subject. A report is a structured way of communicating complex information and can vary in length, complexity and importance. Reports can be:

- short or extended

- formal or informal

- routine or 'one-off'

- internal or external

It all depends on who is going to read it and how important it is. Examples of a less complex **routine report** include:

- a monthly sales report for internal management analysing sales figures by product and region

- a monthly report for management setting out the overtime worked by employees in the various departments of the business

A less formal report may just have a title, date, the name of the person/department that prepared it, the information provided and comments.

Examples of a more complex and formal **'one-off' report** include:

- a **report** to investigate, discuss and decide on specific **policy** issues, for example an assessment of changes to the accounting system, the paying of bonuses, the possibility of exporting products

- a report prepared for a business by outside consultants, eg on health and safety requirements

contents of a formal business report

A more complex formal report will have the following sections (note that they are numbered):

Title Page	
1	Summary (Executive Summary)
2	Introduction
3	Findings
4	Conclusions
5	Recommendations
6	Appendices

Title page

The report will normally be headed up with a single page setting out:

- details of the person/people it is being sent to (including job title)
- the person who has prepared the report (including job title)
- the date
- the title of the report

For example:

> To: Josh Khan, Accounts Manager
>
> From: A Student, Accounts Assistant, Accounts Receivables
>
> Date: 5 February 20-7
>
> REPORT ON OVERDUE CUSTOMER ACCOUNTS

1 Summary

This section is also sometimes known as an **executive summary** because it is written for rapid reading by management (the 'executives'). It may take up less than a page. The summary will be brief and will set out:

- the subject matter of the report – in this case customers who have not settled their accounts on time
- what the report covers – the findings of the investigation into overdue debts
- conclusion(s) of the report – brief details and assessment of the findings
- what the report recommends – identification of the debts that should be written off

2 Introduction

This will state:

- the nature of the task set and the date when it was set
- the person who set the task
- the deadline for the task

See the next page for an example of how the Introduction might read.

---

2 Introduction

2.1 On 30 January a request was made for:

- an investigation into accounts receivable accounts that were outstanding for more than six months later than the due date

- the provision of a list and details of all overdue amounts

2.2 This report was to be completed by 7 February.

Note that the decimal system of numbering is used. This means that this second section of the report is the Introduction and . . .

■ it is given the identifying number '2'

■ the sub-sections of the Introduction are referenced with the numbers '2.1' and '2.2'. If there had been a third it would have been '2.3'.

3 Findings (Main Body)

The third section of the report contains the 'Findings'. This is the **main body** of the report and sets out all the information gathered together as a result of the investigation. It lists sources of information and presents the findings in a clear and logical way.

A table could be incorporated to set out data. If a spreadsheet is used it will give a professional appearance to the report. If the findings include a large amount of data or printouts, they should be included in an Appendix and referred to in the main text.

---

3 Findings

3.1 The information gathered for this report has been taken from:

- the sales ledger

- copies of relevant correspondence relating to the overdue accounts

3.2 A detailed list showing the accounts overdue more than six months is set out below.

---

4 Conclusions

The conclusions should be based entirely on the 'Findings' and should not introduce any other factors or information. This section of the report could begin as follows:

---

4   Conclusions

4.1   The figures and the correspondence in the Findings indicate that it is unlikely that the Finance Department will be able to recover the following customer debts:

      . . . *(a list of the relevant accounts and amounts would be entered)*

---

5 Recommendations

The recommendations are the actions that should be taken as a result of the conclusions reached in the previous section of the report. For example, in the case of the irrecoverable debts:

---

5   Recommendations

5.1   It is recommended that the following accounts should be chased up and Court Action threatened.

Sometimes, if the conclusions are brief and straightforward it makes sense to combine the 'Conclusions' and 'Recommendations' sections.

6 Appendices

This final section of a report will include the reference material which is too bulky to include in the main 'Findings' section. This could include lists of accounts receivable account balances and aged trade receivable analysis.

---

6   Appendices

6.1   Accounts receivable account balances (as at 31 January 20-7).

6.2   Aged trade receivables balances (as at 31 January 20-7).

The diagram below summarises the process of putting a Business Report together.

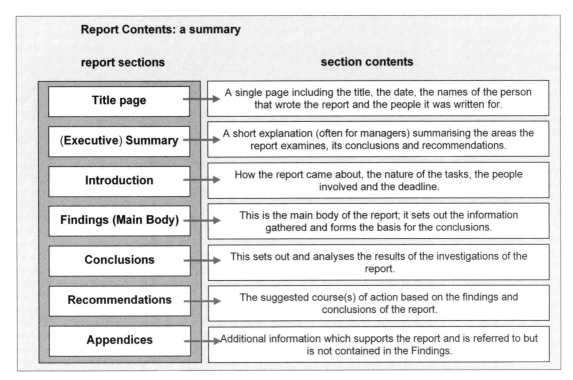

Report Contents: a summary

report sections	section contents
Title page	A single page including the title, the date, the names of the person that wrote the report and the people it was written for.
(Executive) Summary	A short explanation (often for managers) summarising the areas the report examines, its conclusions and recommendations.
Introduction	How the report came about, the nature of the tasks, the people involved and the deadline.
Findings (Main Body)	This is the main body of the report; it sets out the information gathered and forms the basis for the conclusions.
Conclusions	This sets out and analyses the results of the investigations of the report.
Recommendations	The suggested course(s) of action based on the findings and conclusions of the report.
Appendices	Additional information which supports the report and is referred to but is not contained in the Findings.

SPREADSHEETS

what is a spreadsheet?

A spreadsheet can be defined as:

a computer program that organises numbers and text in columns and rows and enables the user to perform numerical calculations

Spreadsheets are very widely used by individuals, businesses and other organisations for a variety of purposes:

- simple and complex calculations

- presentation of numerical data

- construction of graphs and charts based on the numerical data

The basic structure of a spreadsheet is shown below. Its main features are as follows:

- it is set out in rows and columns

- each column is given a consecutive alphabetic reference, ie A,B,C etc

- each row is given a consecutive numeric reference, ie 1,2,3,4,5 etc

- where each column and row intersect is a box known as a 'cell' which is given the reference of the appropriate column and row; in the illustration below cell A2 is highlighted:

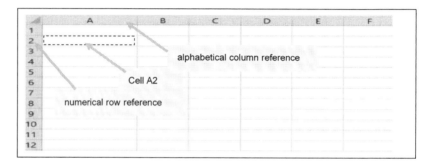

worksheets

Another feature of a spreadsheet file is the use of worksheets. These are the computer equivalent of separate pages used for calculations in a paper-based system. They are accessed by means of tabs at the bottom of a spreadsheet file, as shown below. In this example it is Worksheet 1 which is being shown on the next page. Worksheet 2 can be accessed by clicking on the Sheet 2 tab.

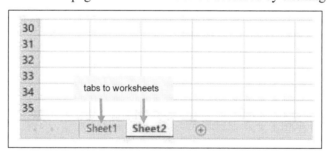

calculations using spreadsheet formulas

One of the major benefits of using spreadsheets in the finance function is its ability to process calculations involving large volumes of numerical data accurately and instantly. In your later AAT studies you will need to be able to set up a spreadsheet using **formulas** for calculations. The main formulas include cell references and symbols, for example:

- addition: =SUM(B4:B13)

- subtraction: =SUM(B5-B4)

- multiplication: =B4*C4

- division: =B4/C4

To put all this into context, examples of formulas for addition and multiplication are explained and illustrated.

addition

In order to create a formula you will need to enter an equals sign (=) in the cell which is going to contain the result, followed by the source cell references and symbols needed for the calculation as follows:

- **simple addition**, use an equals sign followed by the cell references (with numbers) separated by a '+' sign

  =B4+B5+B6

- **addition involving a large number of cells**, eg B4 to B13, use a formula including a ':' symbol:

  =SUM(B4:B13)

This is used on the next page to add up a list of sales expenses by sales reps:

	A	B	C	D	E	F	G
1	ROPER & CO SALES EXPENSES January - June 20-7						
2							
3	Sales person	Jan	Feb	Mar	Apr	May	Jun
4	Adams	746.00					
5	Duffy	202.50					
6	Fanaletto	233.90					
7	Grundy	67.50					
8	Hanwell	193.60					
9	Marsland	726.12					
10	Pamboris	89.00					
11	Simpson	320.50					
12	Thamiayah	728.50					
13	Wong	973.00					
14	TOTAL	=SUM(B4:B13)					

multiplication

In order to create a multiplication formula, enter an equals sign (=) in the cell, which is going to contain the result, followed by the source cell reference, an asterisk '*' and then the number involved in the multiplication. The left-hand illustration below shows the formula for calculation of sales commission due. The commission rate is 15% of sales and so the number entered in the formula is 0.15, which is the result of 15/100. The formula is therefore:

  =B4*0.15

The right-hand illustration below shows the finished result after the formula has been copied into each of the cells in column C.

◇	A	B	C
1	ROPER & CO SALES COMMISSION January 20-7		
2			
3	Sales person	Sales	Commission @ 15%
4	Adams	15060.00	=B4*0.15
5	Duffy	7400.00	
6	Fanaletto	8632.00	
7	Grundy	4529.00	
8	Hanwell	4562.00	
9	Marsland	8481.00	
10	Pamboris	5382.00	

◇	A	B	C
1	ROPER & CO SALES COMMISSION January 20-7		
2			
3	Sales person	Sales	Commission @ 15
4	Adams	15060.00	2259.0
5	Duffy	7400.00	1110.0
6	Fanaletto	8632.00	1294.8
7	Grundy	4529.00	679.3
8	Hanwell	4562.00	684.3
9	Marsland	8481.00	1272.1
10	Pamboris	5382.00	807.3

spreadsheet graphs and charts

One of the other major advantages of using spreadsheets is that they can create graphs and charts from any selected numerical data. These can be used in reports created and presentations made within the finance function. The examples of charts below give a visual representation of trends and proportions.

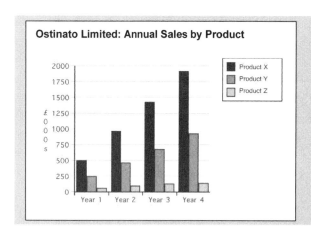

bar chart

This type of chart is made up of vertical bars which show the sales trend of Ostinato Limited over four years.

Each year has a separate bar for each category, the product lines X, Y and Z.

As you can see, the sales are clearly very much on an upwards trend.

Some bar chars just have one single bar for each time period, eg total sales for the year.

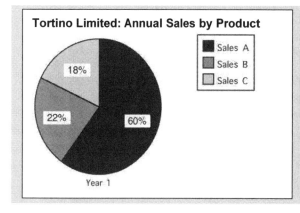

pie chart

This type of chart is circular shaped just like a 'pie'.

Its 'slices' show the proportions of the sales made by Tortino Limited in just one year.

As you can see, the company's most successful product line is Product A.

Unlike a bar chart this type of chart concentrates on showing proportions rather than any trends.

INEFFECTIVE AND INAPPROPRIATE COMMUNICATION

language and style

Written business communication requires straightforward written English. There can be a tendency to write as the spoken word, or as you text, message or post on social media. The result is often an abbreviated form of written English which as you will appreci8 does nt work 2 well on the page.

The test of good written English is that it should be plain and simple, for example:

- use **simple words** instead of complicated ones

- use **short sentences** instead of long ones

- split up the text into manageable **paragraphs**

- use the **active tense** rather than the passive, eg 'the line manager *carries out* regular checks on the petty cash book' rather than 'regular checks *are carried out* on the petty cash book by the line manager'

- **avoid slang** eg 'the manager was really *hacked off*'; you should use the word 'annoyed' instead of 'hacked' to avoid the innocent reader assuming that the manager has suffered some terrible injury

- avoid **abbreviations** such as 'isn't', 'didn't' and write the phrases in full: 'is not' and 'did not'

ineffective communication

We have established the qualities of effective communication. If communication is ineffective it may be because:

- it is not clear and is difficult to understand

- it is too long-winded

- it does not use straightforward language and the meaning can be misinterpreted

- it is incomplete

- it is not accurate

- it has been received too early or too late

- it is not appropriate to the person or people receiving it and it does not meet their needs

- it is not in the most appropriate format

inappropriate communication

Although there are benefits to the use of social media, there is a lot of inappropriate content in circulation, such as embarrassing or provocative photographs and videos (examples include not posting political views and photographs showing work or school logos), the sharing of personal information, cyberbullying and unwanted, targeted, advertising and marketing.

the consequences of ineffective and inappropriate communication

Individuals should be aware that that both ineffective and inappropriate communication can have consequences for both the organisation they represent and for themselves.

- organisations could face:
  - loss of customers
  - damage to reputation
  - bad press
  - loss of profit
  - loss of key personnel
  - threat of legal action
  - penalties and fines
- individual employees could face:
  - disciplinary action
  - loss of financial reward
  - lack of promotion
  - loss of job
  - loss of reputation

**Chapter
Summary**

- Effective communication is essential to the efficient running of an organisation. Any message must be easily understood, correct and communicated on time.

- Communication in an organisation can be **internal** (with colleagues) and **external** (eg with customers). It is important that all external communications, whatever the format, give a **professional image** of the organisation.

- There are many different types of communication, all used for very specific purposes, for example:

  - verbal and written communications

  - paper-based and electronic communications

- The main **verbal communications** are telephone and voicemail messages, discussions in meetings and conference calls.

- The main **written communications** are business letters, notes, reports, emails, texts, messaging, intranet and social media

- **Spreadsheets** are extremely useful in finance as they can carry out complex calculations accurately and quickly; they can also be set up to produce charts and graphs illustrating trends and proportions.

- The importance of effective and appropriate communication must be considered at all times, as ineffective and inappropriate communication can have dire consequences.

business letter	a formal paper document, drawn up in a specific 'house style,' used for a wide range of purposes and normally posted to the recipient
email	a form of electronic communication with a unique set of procedures, different from letter writing
netiquette	the rules for writing emails which must be strictly observed if an organisation is to maintain a professional image
intranet	a computer network for sharing information within organisations
social media	websites and application for technology users to create and share content
note	a simple written message used within an organisation to pass on information, make a request or enable an employee to prepare a verbal communication
business report	a structured document used to communicate complex information and recommendations following an investigation and/or analysis
spreadsheet	a computer program that organises numbers and text in columns and rows forming 'cells' into which data is entered enabling the user to perform numerical calculations
worksheet	separate 'pages' of a spreadsheet accessed by tabs at the bottom of the screen
formulas	numbers, cell references and mathematical symbols entered into a spreadsheet cell in order to carry out calculations, the result of which will be shown in that cell
bar chart	a chart which sets out a series of bars, the height of which indicates the extent of the value that varies – useful for illustrating trends
pie chart	a circle divided into sectors to represent in the correct proportion the parts of a whole – like a pie divided into 'slices' which shows the sections that make up a whole

Activities

6.1 Which **one** of the following four options is the most important for communicating a message? Tick the correct option.

(a)	The message must be clear and in writing	
(b)	The message must be clear and correct	
(c)	The message must be clear and on time	
(d)	The message must be clear, correct and on time	

6.2 Which **two** of the following are qualities of an effective communication? Tick the correct options.

(a)	It needs to be made as quickly as possible	
(b)	It must be made within an appropriate timescale	
(c)	It needs to be made using language appropriate to the situation	
(d)	It needs to be made using formal and complex business language	

6.3 A customer sends your business a rude email containing inappropriate words, complaining about poor customer service. What should you do? Tick the most appropriate response.

(a)	Ignore the email completely because the customer is so rude	
(b)	Reply using similar language	
(c)	Reply politely with apologies	
(d)	Reply politely and tell the customer that it is unacceptable to use bad language	

6.4 Its or It's? Study the four sentences below and tick the **two** correct options.

(a)	Its rubbish weather today	
(b)	It's rubbish weather today	
(c)	I do not like this film; it's not one of the best Bond films	
(d)	I do not like this film; its not one of the best Bond films	

6.5 'There', 'their' or 'they're'? Study the three sentences below and if you think any of them are wrong, write the correct word in the right-hand column.

(a)	Politicians are corrupt. Their all the same	
(b)	The students forgot there calculators for the assessment	
(c)	They're are sensible students who brought calculators	

6.6 A senior colleague has been compiling a report for management. He has written each section of the report in a separate Word file and has emailed you seven files which appear to be in the wrong order. The file names are shown below in the boxes on the left. You are to write the file names in the boxes on the right in the correct order, starting with the first file name at the top.

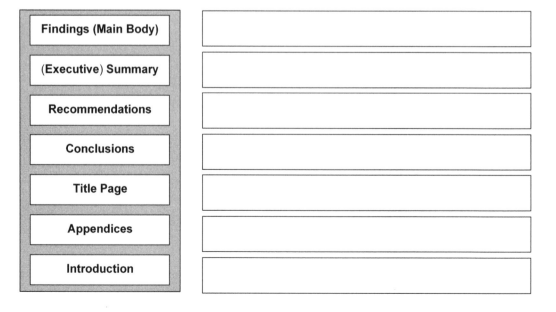

Findings (Main Body)	
(Executive) Summary	
Recommendations	
Conclusions	
Title Page	
Appendices	
Introduction	

6.7 You have been passed the following draft letter (to a Miss Coleman) to check. The letter concerns Order No 239847224. It has not yet been signed.

There are six major errors which could include wrong spellings, bad grammar or wrong use of words.

You are to:

(a) Identify the six incorrect words and enter them in the left-hand column of the table below.

(b) Enter your correction of these six words on the appropriate line in the right-hand column of the table below.

Dear Mrs Colman,

Refund for faulty goods (Order Ref 239847244)

We are sorry that you are dissappointed with the goods you ordered from us on 5 September.

They're are two possible solutions to the problem: we can make a refund on your credit card account or issue you with a credit note.

Please let us know which course of action you would like us to take.

Yours faithfully,

Incorrect word	Correction

6.8 Your name is Jamie and you work as an assistant in the Accounts Department of Frankie's Fashionware and have been passed the draft email (shown below) to complete.

The email is a request to Laura Wood (l.wood@frankiesfashionware.co.uk), an assistant in the Sales Department, to provide details of 'St Tropez shades (code 9424)' sold during the month of June. You need the information by 9 July. **You are to:**

(a) Insert the email address of the recipient in the appropriate box.

(b) Complete the remaining boxes (they are numbered for reference) with the most appropriate words or phrases from the lists shown below (also numbered for reference).

From	j.mason@frankiesfashionware.co.uk
To	
Subject	[1]

Hi Laura

Please send me the quantity of [2] sold

during the month of [3] . We need this information to carry

out a costing exercise. I need the information, please, by [4] .

Many thanks and kind regards

Jamie

Accounts Department

Option Lists

Pick one word or phrase for each numbered box from the following numbered lists:

1. Sales data for June, June data, Tropez data, Shades

2. St Tropez shades (code 9242), St Tropez shades (code 9424), St Tropez shades

3. July, August, June, September

4. 9 June, 2 August, 9 July, 9 August

6.9   The following two notes were written within the finance function of a business. In each case identify and write down two important elements that are missing.

(a)

To Jez Warlock,

Order Processing

Please remember to allow Roper Ltd an extra trade discount on their invoices this month.

04.04.-7   10.30

answer

(b)

TELEPHONE MESSAGE

TO   Karin Schmidt, Accounts

FROM   H Khan, Sales

DATE

TIME   12.30

Please ring RF Electronics – they are complaining that they have not received a credit note. Please treat urgently – they are not happy!

HK

answer

6.10   Give examples of three situations in which an employee might write down notes in preparation for a conversation they have to make or a presentation they have to give.

1	
2	
3	

7 Planning and managing your work

this chapter covers...

This chapter explains the need for a person working in an organisation to be able to plan and manage their work in order to help achieve the objectives of the organisation.

The principles set out here apply not just to the finance function but to all areas of the organisation.

An employee must be able to:

- *work to achieve the objectives of the organisation – for example customer satisfaction and profitability*

- *work in line with the procedures set out by the organisation*

- *manage the workload by identifying the different types of tasks involved*

- *prioritise these tasks and meet deadlines that have been set*

- *use appropriate planning aids such as diaries, 'to do' lists, electronic planners, action plans and schedules to help with this process*

- *understand the importance of communicating clearly and promptly with management and other employees during the completion of tasks and also when deadlines are in danger of not being achieved*

- *know what to do if things do not go to plan, priorities change and rescheduling becomes necessary*

THE INDIVIDUAL AND THE ORGANISATION

working effectively in finance

It is important that employees learn to treat the workplace as an environment in which they have a sense of responsibility for what they do, for example:

■ the everyday tasks that they have to carry out

■ working with others to achieve common objectives set by the organisation

'Working effectively' means getting the result that you want. In sport an effective defence prevents the opposing team scoring goals; in the workplace an **effective working environment** will result in the achievement of the objectives of the organisation – for example, a motivated workforce, sales and profit targets achieved or exceeded.

Note that 'efficient' is not the same as 'effective'. It means getting the job done with the minimum waste of effort and resources. This is, of course, an important objective in any organisation. But note that an **efficient working environment** will not always be 'effective'. A line manager, for example, may be ruthlessly efficient in saving time and money, but the workforce may be fed up with them to the extent that levels of performance will drastically reduce. The working environment will become less 'effective'.

The ideal working environment, therefore, is one that **balances effectiveness and efficiency**. The job is done well with the minimum wastage of effort and resources.

employees and objectives

The common objectives of an organisation may include:

■ customer satisfaction – making the customer the main focus of the organisation

■ profitability – which should benefit employees, owners and customers

■ being environmentally friendly – reducing wastage of natural resources, eg energy and paper

In order to achieve these objectives, organisations promote:

■ customer care schemes

■ profit-sharing schemes

■ 'green' schemes to cut down on wastage, eg of energy and paper

These objectives will affect the way in which employees are required to carry out their day-to-day tasks.

The example below shows how a Customer Care scheme used by a financial services company sets very specific targets for the performance of workplace tasks. When an assistant sorts out a customer query, it is not just a case of 'that's another one out of the way' but 'I got a buzz of satisfaction in showing that our organisation cares about its customers.'

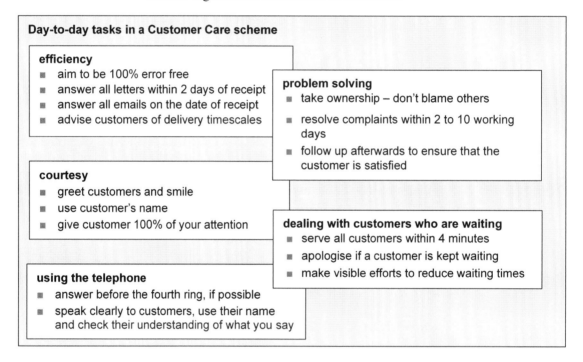

Day-to-day tasks in a Customer Care scheme

efficiency
- aim to be 100% error free
- answer all letters within 2 days of receipt
- answer all emails on the date of receipt
- advise customers of delivery timescales

problem solving
- take ownership – don't blame others
- resolve complaints within 2 to 10 working days
- follow up afterwards to ensure that the customer is satisfied

courtesy
- greet customers and smile
- use customer's name
- give customer 100% of your attention

dealing with customers who are waiting
- serve all customers within 4 minutes
- apologise if a customer is kept waiting
- make visible efforts to reduce waiting times

using the telephone
- answer before the fourth ring, if possible
- speak clearly to customers, use their name and check their understanding of what you say

complying with organisational procedures

The way in which employees tackle tasks is often set down in written sets of **procedures**. Larger organisations are likely to have manuals which give guidance; smaller organisations may have written 'checklists' compiled by experienced staff. Examples of tasks in a finance context which will have set procedures for the tasks carried out include:

- checking and paying supplier invoices
- dealing with petty cash
- dealing with amounts being paid into the bank
- processing payroll
- backing up data processed on computer systems

THE NEED TO PRIORITISE TASKS

An employee may have sets of instructions and procedures to learn when doing a job. The day-to-day work will involve a wide variety of tasks competing for the employee's time. These may be **routine** or **non-routine**, **urgent** or **non-urgent**. The employee must develop the skills needed to identify and prioritise the tasks that need to be done. We will examine the techniques and aids available to the employee to help with this.

keeping to the job description

An employee needs to know:

▪ what tasks need to be done

▪ what tasks the employee is able to do

These are not necessarily the same. Employees should be given a **job description** which sets out exactly what the employee is expected to be able to do. It may be that a line manager puts pressure onto an employee to carry out tasks which the employee is not qualified or able to do. The employee may think 'promotion here we come!' but also may get in a mess and make mistakes for which he or she should not really be held responsible.

One golden rule is therefore to look at your job description and know what you have to do and what limits there are to your range of activities.

identifying types of tasks

The next golden rule is to be able to identify exactly what tasks have to be completed and to identify what type of tasks they are, because this will affect the order in which they are carried out.

There will normally be a number of different types of tasks in a finance office:

▪ **routine tasks**

These are everyday tasks such as reading the post and emails, checking invoices, inputting data, sending standard letters and emails, answering telephone queries, photocopying and filing. They may not be particularly challenging, but their efficient completion is important to the smooth running of the office.

▪ **non-routine ('ad hoc') tasks**

'Ad hoc' simply means 'for this situation'. These are the unexpected tasks such as helping with one-off projects, working out of the office on a special assignment, or helping to clear up after the washroom has flooded. These may hold up your normal routine work.

Routine tasks are easy to plan for because they are predictable. **Non-routine tasks** cannot be planned for, and they can sometimes cause problems.

Tasks may be **urgent** and may be **important**. These are not the same thing:

- **urgent tasks**

  These are tasks which have to be done by a specific pressing deadline: the manager may need a spreadsheet immediately for a meeting currently taking place; customer statements may have to go out in tonight's post.

- **important tasks**

  These are tasks for which you have been given personal responsibility. They may be part of your normal routine and other people depend on their successful completion, or they may have been delegated to you because your line manager thinks you are capable of completing them.

working out the priorities

Prioritising tasks means deciding the order of the tasks. Which one first? Which one last? The two main factors involved in the decision are **urgency** and **importance**. The guide to the basic order of priority is shown below.

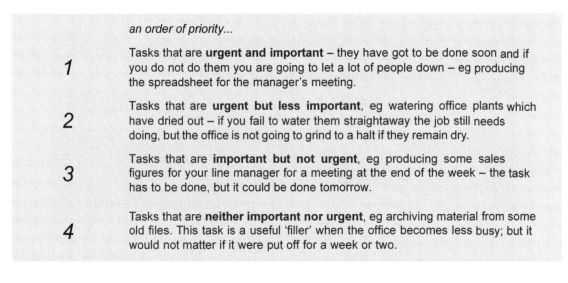

an order of priority...

1 Tasks that are **urgent and important** – they have got to be done soon and if you do not do them you are going to let a lot of people down – eg producing the spreadsheet for the manager's meeting.

2 Tasks that are **urgent but less important**, eg watering office plants which have dried out – if you fail to water them straightaway the job still needs doing, but the office is not going to grind to a halt if they remain dry.

3 Tasks that are **important but not urgent**, eg producing some sales figures for your line manager for a meeting at the end of the week – the task has to be done, but it could be done tomorrow.

4 Tasks that are **neither important nor urgent**, eg archiving material from some old files. This task is a useful 'filler' when the office becomes less busy; but it would not matter if it were put off for a week or two.

On the next page is a Case Study illustrating these principles. Note in the various situations the importance of the need to **communicate** openly with work colleagues and management when there are problems to be solved.

Case Study

FLICK'S DAY – WORKING OUT THE PRIORITIES

Flick works as an assistant in the finance office of the Liverpool head office of Estro PLC, a company that makes vacuum cleaners. Her main job is to process incoming sales orders. She is supervised by her line manager Josie Khan.

She is not having a good week and seems stressed by the workload she has been given. It is Thursday 6 February and things are getting no better.

She has written down her tasks on various bits of paper and has stuck post-it notes on the side of her computer screen, marking them 'Remember!' Her colleague, Kirsty, has written notes to her. She also has her daily routine sheet which came with her job description.

These are all shown below.

SALES ORDER PROCESSING: DAILY ROUTINE

1   Collect mail, open, sort and refer where necessary

2   Open email and deal with queries - refer where necessary

3   Check incoming sales orders and debit notes

4   Check sales orders with credit control lists

5   Batch and process sales orders on computer

6   Print sales invoices and credit notes

7   Check printed documents

8   Agree batch total with computer day book summary

9   Pass invoices and credit notes for checking against order documentation

10   File copy invoices, credit notes and order documentation

11   Answer customer queries - refer where necessary

These are the notes received from Kirsty, Flick's colleague:

Flick – Finance Manager wants January sales Figures asap!

Kirsty 6 Feb 9.30

Flick – we are moving the computers at 2.00 Thursday afternoon – can you help?

Kirsty

These are the 'Remember!' post-it notes Flick has stuck on the side of her computer screen:

REMEMBER!

Get instant coffee for staff kitchen. Ordinary and decaf! Both jars now empty

REMEMBER!

4 FEB

Josie wants printouts of top 10 customer activity reports by end of Friday.

REMEMBER!

Old customer sales files need moving to separate filing drawer some time.

How is Flick going to work out her priorities?

solution

Flick takes a short morning break to discuss her various tasks with her line manager, Josie. At Josie's suggestion she thinks about the priorities involved and classifies the tasks according to how urgent they are and how important they are. She starts by prioritising the non-routine/unexpected tasks:

urgent and important tasks

- The Finance Manager wants the January sales figures straightaway.

- The computers have to be moved at 2.00 pm that day.

urgent and less important tasks

- The staff kitchen needs more coffee.

important and non-urgent tasks

- The top 10 customer activity reports are required for Friday.

less important and non-urgent tasks

- The old customer sales files need moving to a separate filing drawer.

The non-routine tasks are fairly easily prioritised, as seen above, although there was some uncertainty over whether the staff coffee or the customer printouts had greater priority! But Flick's problem was how to combine the non-routine tasks with the big pile of routine paperwork she had to get through that day. Then there was the filing to do and customers on the telephone with complicated queries.

Josie, her line manager, suggests that she should deal with her tasks in the following order:

1 urgent and important tasks – the January sales figures, shifting the computers

2 important routine tasks – these include processing and checking documentation, answering customer queries

3 urgent and less important tasks – it will not take long to get some more coffee

4 important and non-urgent tasks – the printouts for the next day (Friday)

5 less important and non-urgent tasks – filing (daily filing and shifting old files)

Josie also suggests that Flick compiles a prioritised 'To Do' list of all her non-routine tasks. She can then tick off the items as she does them. This will replace all the notes and Post-it stickers she has all over her desk. It can also be updated as she is asked to carry out new non-routine tasks.

FLICK'S 'TO DO' LIST

1   January sales figures for the Finance Manager.

2   Thursday 2.00 pm move computers.

3   Coffee - get jars of ordinary <u>and</u> decaf at lunch time.

4   Print out top 10 customer activity reports for Josie, Friday.

5   Move old customer sales files to new drawer, as and when.

USING PLANNING AIDS

The Case Study on the last few pages has shown how an employee has become more effective by becoming more organised and prioritising tasks. The Post-it notes are important in the process, but they are only a start. There are a number of planning aids available to help with organisation, time planning and prioritisation in an accounts office. These include:

- written 'To Do' lists – as seen above

- diaries

- calendars and wall planners

- electronic planners

- schedules

- action plans

'To Do' lists

Making lists of things 'to do' is very common both at work and at home, ranging from the type of list shown above to the very basic family shopping list. It is the organised person, however, who writes these lists on an ongoing basis, possibly daily, incorporating actions which have not been ticked off on the previous day in a new list. In other words, tasks that have not been done are carried forward onto a new list. 'To do' lists can be written on paper, or on electronic devices such as work computers.

'To do' lists may be subdivided to show the priorities of the tasks to be done. Look at the example below.

'TO DO' List   1 April

urgent stuff

1   Aged debtors schedules for the Finance Manager for today.

2   Sales summaries for Costings section for today.

3   Get March statements in the post today.

non-urgent

1   Print out activity reports for overseas customers.

2   Set up spreadsheet for regional sales analysis.

3   Look into venues for staff evening out.

---

diaries

The diary organises tasks in terms of time sequence. They are very useful planning aids and ensure – if they are efficiently kept – that tasks and events do not clash. Diaries can be paper-based or electronic. They can be individual diaries or office or 'section' diaries used for a group of employees.

The traditional paper-based diary with a week to view can be used alongside 'To do' lists as an efficient way of time planning and prioritising.

The diary shown below is kept by a line manager.

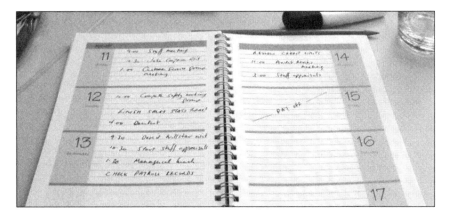

Calendars and wall planners – often fixed to the wall – are useful visual guides to events and processes taking place in an accounting office, for example:

■ ongoing projects, eg installation of a new computer network

■ routine activities, eg end-of-month statements, payroll

■ staff training, eg work-shadowing and coaching

■ and most important of all – holidays

Calendars and wall planners are essentially **team** planning devices.

electronic planning software

The functions of a diary, calendar and prioritisation planner are usefully combined in computer 'planner' software which is available in one form or another on many computers. These provide the functions of:

■ diary

■ 'to do' lists

■ task prioritisation

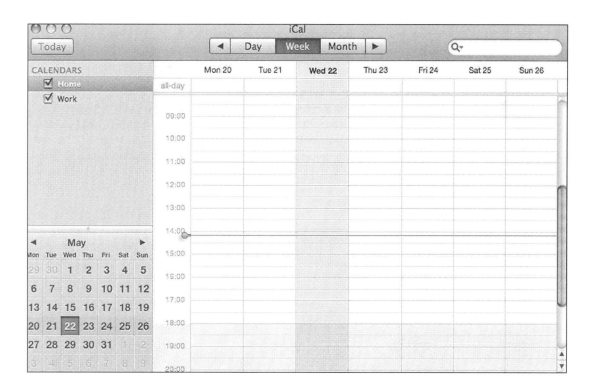

planning schedules

Planning schedules are rather more complex planning devices which deal with situations such as projects where:

- some tasks *have* to follow on from each other – to give a simple example, you have to boil the water before making a cup of coffee. These are known as **critical** activities; you cannot achieve what you want without doing them in sequence

- some tasks are **non-critical** – they are important, but the timing is not so crucial – you will have to put coffee in the cup, but you can do it while the kettle is boiling or even at the beginning of the day if you want

So whether you are making coffee or planning a new computer system for the accounting department, the principles remain the same. Organisations often use a visual representation of the tasks in the form of horizontal bars set against a time scale to help with the planning. These can be drawn up manually, or on a computer using dedicated software.

action plans

An **action plan** is a plan which will:

- define each activity

- record start and completion dates for individual activities

- state who is responsible for carrying out each activity

- in some cases state the cost of each activity

This form of plan is a form of checklist which can be regularly monitored and amended as required. Plans rarely go according 'to plan'. Spreadsheets are often used for setting out action plans because they can be easily amended and printed out in revised form. An extract from an action plan is shown below.

marketing action plan

Product 247G - launch date April

Month	Activity	Person in charge	completed	budget £	actual £
Feb	Book press adverts - trade magazines	RP	6 Feb	5,600	5,750
Feb	Leaflet design	HG	12 Feb	1,200	1,200
Feb	Catalogue design	HG	12 Feb	2,400	2,750
March	Leaflet printing	GF		12,000	
March	Catalogue printing	GF		34,500	
March	Press releases	DD		100	
April	Public launch on 1 April	DD		50,000	

DEALING WITH DEADLINES

what to do when you cannot meet deadlines

Things never go quite according to plan. The unexpected can occur and what seems like a quiet productive day can turn into a stressful time, full of awkward decisions. For a finance assistant an important aspect of working is therefore **keeping the line manager advised** of what is going on and communicating any problems that arise. The manager will want to be the first to know. If deadlines are not being met, changes will have to be made:

- tasks may change in order of priority

- tasks may have to be delegated

- tasks may have to be delayed

consequences of poor performance at work

Non-completion or a bad standard of work can have serious consequences. If you work as a finance assistant, or a member of a work 'team', it is important to realise what will happen if:

- work is not completed to the necessary standard

- work is completed late

- work is not completed at all

Not only will the individual feel a failure, but colleagues will be let down and the department will get a bad name. If the public are involved, the reputation of the business may suffer. In these days of online reviews of competitive products and services, a poor review can seriously affect sales.

Here are some examples of how an accounting department could be let down and the reputation of the business affected:

- sales invoices not being checked properly, resulting in customers being overcharged

- statements of account not being sent out which will result in customers not paying their invoices on time and the business becoming short of cash

- careless handling of customer credit card details and the bad publicity which follows if fraudulent transactions result

consequences of good performance at work

If, on the other hand, an employee produces a good standard of work and meets deadlines, this will have a positive effect on colleagues, the team and the whole business. It will also enable the employee to appreciate that his or her contribution to the organisation is valued and important.

The following Case Study describes how a finance assistant faces a number of problems during a working day. It explains how she deals with the problems by communicating with management and colleagues, prioritising and rescheduling her tasks and making a success of the day.

FLICK'S DAY – CHANGING THE PRIORITIES

Flick works as an assistant in the finance office of the Liverpool head office of Estro PLC, a company that makes vacuum cleaners.

The Case Study which starts on page 155 showed how Flick prioritised her tasks on one working day – Thursday 6 February.

In this Case Study we will see how she copes with unexpected events on that day by changing the priorities of her tasks and asking for help from managerial staff where appropriate.

To recap on what Flick had planned for Thursday:

1   The urgent tasks were to provide the January sales figures for the Finance Manager and to help with moving the computers in the afternoon.

2   Flick had planned to get some jars of coffee at lunchtime.

3   There was the normal daily sales order processing work and filing to be done.

4   Flick also had to provide some customer activity printouts for the following day and had been asked to move some filing records.

Flick's problems

Flick was faced with a number of problems as soon as she got to work on the Thursday. These meant that her carefully thought out work plan was in trouble and would have to be revised. The problems were:

1   **09.30**. Her colleague, Kirsty, who helped her with her sales order processing work had to go home sick. There was a trainee working on the invoicing as well, but Flick doubted if this trainee could cope with the extra work involved.

2   **10.00**. Flick saw from Kirsty's note that she had to give the Finance Manager the January sales figures 'as soon as possible'. This seemed a bit vague. Did it mean during the morning, or would later in the day be OK?

3   **11.30**. Flick's printer jammed and a long run of invoices was ruined. She could not seem to get it to work again.

4   **12.00**. The Human Resources Manager phoned through to ask if she could 'pop in' to see her at 1.45. Was she free then? Flick knew that she had to move the computers at 2.00.

5   **12.30**. Flick realised that she was going to have to work for most of her lunch break. What about the coffee she was supposed to be getting?

Flick was faced with a number of situations which clearly meant that her work plan was going to be disrupted and would have to be revised. But how was she to do this? She obviously needed to communicate with both management and colleagues about what should be done. Some of the decisions would have to be made by the management.

09.30 Kirsty away off sick

Kirsty's absence would mean that Kirsty's routine processing work would have to be done by someone else – either Flick (who was busy anyway) or the trainee – unless it could be left until the next day. Flick would need to assess how much work there was and then speak to the line manager, Josie. The line manager said to Flick, 'Do what you can, concentrating on orders from the important customers. The rest will have to wait. I don't think the trainee can be left on her own yet'. Flick was not too happy about this because she was very busy herself. She would have to put some of her other tasks back in order of priority.

10.00 the figures for the Finance Manager

Flick realised that this was a priority job. To clarify what 'as soon as possible' really meant, she emailed the Finance Manager who replied that the figures would be needed by lunchtime that day for a meeting in the afternoon. This job remained top priority.

11.30 printer jam

The printer jam had to be referred to the line manager who called in the maintenance engineer. Flick knew that the invoices would have to be printed that day, so she arranged to print them on another printer through the network. She lost valuable time in sorting out this problem and only got back to work at 11.50, by which time she was getting really stressed.

12.00 Human Resources Manager

Flick realised that the 1.45 appointment with the Human Resources Manager would clash with having to move the computers. The request, however, came from a senior manager and took priority over most other tasks. Flick referred the problem to her line manager who said it would be okay for Flick to go to the appointment. Flick was secretly quite pleased to miss lugging the computers about.

12.30 coffee?

Flick realised that she would have to work through some of her lunch hour, which meant that she would not be able to get the coffee. She explained this to Jack, another colleague, who agreed to get the coffee for her.

17.00 end of the day review . . .

Flick is in good spirits because she has had a productive afternoon. Her work targets for the day have largely been completed, despite the changes of plan. The sales figures have been given to the Finance Manager and much of the sales processing work has been completed. Flick has had an interview with the Human Resources Manager and even arranged for the coffee to be bought.

How has this all been achieved? Flick has successfully reworked her priorities and made the most of her resources by using her communication skills, delegating tasks and consulting management where appropriate.

Chapter Summary

■ An individual working independently should be able to combine efficiency and effectiveness when planning the daily workload.

■ Employees working independently should develop the skill of prioritising tasks and be able to plan their activities accordingly.

■ A 'rule of thumb' order of priority for tasks is:

1   urgent and important tasks

2   urgent and less important tasks

3   important and not urgent tasks

4   tasks that are neither urgent nor important

■ Employees should be familiar with different types of planning aids and construct their own 'To Do' lists and diaries and be familiar with electronic planning aids. They should be aware of planning aids such as project planning schedules and action plans, but they will not have to draw them up.

■ Employees should understand the need to monitor the progress of a work plan over time in order to meet deadlines, and have the flexibility to be able to re-prioritise if unexpected events happen.

■ Employees should be able to communicate with management if they need help; they should also be able to delegate tasks if the need arises, maintaining confidentiality where appropriate.

Key Terms		
	effective	getting the result that you want
	efficient	a task done with the minimum of wastage of effort and resources
	non-routine task	an unexpected task which is not part of the everyday work of an employee
	urgent task	a task which has a pressing deadline
	important task	a task which an employee needs to complete and which significantly affects other employees
	'To Do' list	a checklist of tasks, made by an individual, which can be ticked off when they are completed
	schedule	a chart used for planning projects which organises tasks in terms of time and priority
	action plan	a checklist for a series of activities, listing the main tasks, when they have to be done and by whom
	prioritising	planning tasks in order of urgency and importance

Activities

7.1 You work in an accounts office and together with a full-time colleague work on the order processing and invoicing. One morning your colleague telephones in to say that because of a major domestic problem she is unable to come in that day. Your line manager has said that she can have the day off. The colleague has a pile of purchase orders on her desk which need checking before processing and invoicing, but the line manager, who is a bit stressed that morning, has not asked you to do anything about your colleague's work.

Select and tick the most appropriate action to be taken.

(a)	Carry on with your own work and hope that your colleague will come in tomorrow and clear up the backlog	
(b)	Process your colleague's work as quickly as possible before doing your own tasks. This may mean missing out some of the routine checks that are normally made	
(c)	Carry on with your own work until you have the opportunity to refer the problem to your line manager when she is free	
(d)	Refer the problem to the Senior Finance Manager and say that your line manager is too stressed to deal with the problem	

7.2 You will encounter a variety of tasks in an accounts office. They can be classified as follows:

urgent **non-urgent** **one-off 'ad hoc'**

Complete the following table with the correct classification of task from the above three terms.

Your line manager asks you for the balances of your top 20 customer accounts. She needs the information for a meeting that morning.	
Your line manager asks you to provide information from the office for the accountants who are coming in next week to audit the accounts. You have never done this before as this is normally a senior colleague's responsibility.	
Your colleague reminds you that it is your turn to get the milk from Tesco Express and remarks that the milk has run out.	

7.3 Prioritising tasks involves placing workplace tasks in a specific order. One method of task classification uses the following categories of task:

important but not urgent tasks　　**neither important nor urgent tasks**

urgent and important tasks　　**urgent but less important tasks**

You are to complete the table below by:

(a) entering these four categories in the table below in the order in which you would carry them out

(b) choosing a reason for the placing of each category of task from the following options:

－　　sending round a suggestion list for a staff social

－　　if you don't do this task very soon you are going to let a lot of people down

－　　setting up a spreadsheet for a meeting in a week's time

－　　your manager asks you to turn down the heating

Category of task	Choice of task

7.4　There are a number of planning aids that might be found in an accounting office:

action plan　　　**'to do' list**　　　**diary**　　　**wall planner**

Complete the following table with the appropriate planning aid for each situation.

An employee's personal record of tasks and events over a long period of time.	
A detailed plan which involves a number of people and interrelated tasks and events for a specific purpose over a period of time.	
An annual guide which can be used to display staff holidays and external training courses.	
An employee's daily personal record of tasks to be done in the short term.	

7.5   You are a part-time Accounts Assistant employed by Froyd Limited, a printing business. Your main task is to process the payroll, but you also deal with checking incoming payments, preparing payments to suppliers and dealing with petty cash and the petty cash book.

Your working hours are 09.00 to 13.00 Monday to Friday.

You normally attend the weekly staff meeting at 11.00 every Wednesday.

Most employees are salaried and are paid monthly by direct bank transfer (BACS). Their salaries are processed on the last Wednesday of the month and reach their bank account on the last Friday of the month.

Some casual workers have chosen to be paid weekly by BACS and their salaries are processed every Wednesday and reach the bank account every Friday.

Other casual employees are still paid weekly in cash. The payroll for these employees is processed every Wednesday and paid every Friday. One of your jobs is to go to the bank on Thursday to pick up the cash to make up the pay packets for distribution on Friday. At the same time you also pick up from the bank the notes and coins needed to top up the petty cash.

Your normal routine during the week is set out on the schedule below.

Task description	Scheduling of tasks		Time taken for task
	Day	**Time**	
Process payments received	Monday	9.00	4 hours
Process payments made to suppliers and petty cash payments	Tuesday	9.00	4 hours
Process the payroll (BACS and cash)	Wednesday	9.00	3 hours
Update and balance the petty cash book	Thursday	9.00	2 hours
Visit bank to pick up cash wages and petty cash	Thursday	11.00	1 hour
Check that the cash and petty cash box are locked in the safe	Thursday	12.00	1 hour
Make up cash pay packets and distribute payslips for all employees	Friday	9.00	3 hours

On the last Wednesday in July you and your car are involved in a minor road accident on the way to work. Nobody is hurt but the driver of the other car is not very cooperative and as a result you do not get into the office until 12.00.

The Accounts Manager is very sympathetic as you are a bit shaken up, but he points out that both the weekly and monthly payroll must meet their deadlines as all the staff will need paying on Friday. He suggests that you prioritise what you have to do for the rest of the week. He has agreed to let you work additional hours on Thursday afternoon so that you can ensure that all the tasks are completed.

(a) Using the table below, write a 'to do' list for the rest of Wednesday morning, Thursday and Friday by listing the tasks in order of completion. Write the task descriptions in the column on the right. Choose from the following tasks:

    Make up cash pay packets and distribute payslips for all employees

    Update and balance the petty cash book

    Deal with payments made to suppliers and petty cash payments

    Process the payroll (BACS and cash)

    Check that the cash and petty cash box are locked in the safe

    Visit the bank to pick up cash wages and petty cash top up

    Process payments received

WEDNESDAY/THURSDAY/FRIDAY 'TO DO' LIST (in order of completion)	
Task 1	
Task 2	
Task 3	
Task 4	
Task 5	

(b) If you **do not** carry out the instructions of the Accounts Manager there might be problems. Indicate below with a tick in the appropriate column whether the following outcomes could have serious consequences for Froyd Ltd or not.

		Serious	**Not serious**
(a)	The staff may not get paid on time		
(b)	The cash from the bank may not get locked away		
(c)	Petty cash reimbursements may be delayed		
(d)	Suppliers may not get paid on time		
(e)	Minor office duties may not get done		

Ethics, sustainability and corporate social responsibility

this chapter covers...

This chapter covers three areas which affect both employers and employees working in business: ethics, sustainability and corporate social responsibility.

■ **Ethics** in the workplace involves knowing about and practising basic principles of good and acceptable behaviour at work:

- acting with honesty and fairness

- acting without bias

- behaving in a professional way and developing professional knowledge

- maintaining confidentiality

The AAT Code of Professional Ethics must be complied with by all members.

■ **Sustainability** is a general term which is used to cover a wide range of activities which benefit employees, society and the environment, for example:

- making a profit which benefits society by providing work opportunities

- energy conservation (eg cycle to work schemes, car sharing)

- recycling of waste and other materials (eg paper, plastics)

- helping the community (eg sports sponsorship, charity events)

■ **Corporate social responsibility (CSR)** is a term which describes the various policies adopted by an individual business to put the principles of sustainability into practice.

ETHICS IN THE WORKPLACE

a definition

Ethics in the workplace can be defined as:

'the moral principles or standards that govern the conduct of the members of an organisation'.

In other words, ethics affect the way in which employees should behave, both in the workplace and when representing their organisation outside the workplace. As you will see from this, employees do not 'switch off' ethical behaviour when they leave work. Not only do they have to behave in an ethical way in a finance department, they have to have the interests of the organisation in mind when at home talking to the family and when out socially with friends who may happen to have a commercial interest in the organisation, for example as a customer or as a supplier.

ethical principles

Many professions have their own written Code of Ethics. AAT has a Code of Professional Ethics, which is based on **fundamental ethical principles**, which are the rules that guide ethical behaviour.

There are five fundamental ethical principles which are stated in the AAT Code of Professional Ethics. They are:

- integrity
- objectivity
- professional competence and due care
- confidentiality
- professional behaviour

We will examine each one of these principles in turn.

integrity

The Code defines integrity as:

The principle of integrity imposes an obligation on all members to be straightforward and honest in professional relationships. Integrity also implies fair dealing and truthfulness.

Employees in a finance function should always act honestly and be fair; they should:

- be **straightforward** – respect and obey rules and procedures
- be **honest** – they should not cover up the truth, fiddle the books, or allow anything to pass through the accounting system which they know has not been checked

■ be **truthful** – they should not tell lies, falsify or 'fudge' figures, or mislead customers and suppliers with false information, eg prices, discounts

Here are some examples of unethical behaviour:

not being honest or fair

1　A Finance Manager takes his wife on a holiday trip to Paris and charges the expenses to his employer.
Verdict: he is not honest

2　An Accounts Assistant buys herself and some friends some sandwiches and coffee at the local Costa cafe and uses the receipt to reclaim the money from petty cash, stating that it was an expense for 'entertaining customers'.
Verdict: she is not honest or truthful

objectivity

The Code defines objectivity as:

The principle of objectivity imposes an obligation on all members not to compromise their professional or business judgement because of bias, conflict of interest or the undue influence of others.

Employees in a finance function should:

■ practise **fair dealing** – they should treat everyone (eg customers and suppliers) on an equal basis

An employee should **not**:

■ get involved in a **conflict of interest** – a situation where professional judgement is affected because the employee could benefit personally from a transaction

■ get involved in a situation where someone is putting **undue influence** on an employee to do something that is dishonest and 'against the rules'

Here are some further examples of unethical behaviour:

not acting with objectivity

1　An Accounts Manager lets a customer pay invoices late because the customer is his next-door neighbour and he owes him a favour.
Verdict: this a case of conflict of interest

2　A Finance Manager promises to recommend an assistant for promotion if the assistant keeps quiet about the fact that he has found out that the Manager takes his wife to Paris on company expenses.
Verdict: the Manager is exerting undue influence over the assistant

professional competence and due care

The Code defines professional competence and due care as:

The principle of professional competence and due care imposes the following obligations on members:

- *to maintain professional knowledge and skill at the level required to ensure that clients or employers receive competent professional service; and*

- *to act diligently in accordance with applicable technical and professional standards when providing professional services*

Professional competence means achieving a level of knowledge and skills needed for working at a particular level in the workplace – the more senior the employee, the greater the knowledge and skills that will be needed.

Due care means that the employee must take the required level of care appropriate to the task that is being done. In other words an employee in a finance function must provide a competent and 'professional' service.

Professional competence and due care requires that an employee should:

- act **professionally** – this means carrying out a task according to instructions, carefully, thoroughly and on time

- use **sound judgement** in applying professional knowledge

- know when to **refuse to carry out an area of work** (eg payroll processing) if the employee does not have the necessary knowledge or skills

- plan career progression through **CPD (Continuing Professional Development)**, a programme of qualifications, internal courses and expanding experience

Here are some examples of the wrong type of behaviour:

breaches of professional competence and due care

1 A Finance Line Manager has been asked to take responsibility for the Payroll Section for a few months to cover maternity leave. She has no real experience of this area of the accounting system, but agrees to the request because she is looking for promotion.

Verdict: the Line Manager is not taking notice of the requirement for professional competence – she may not know what she is doing.

2 A Finance Assistant needs to prepare a spreadsheet showing up-to-date financial figures for the Finance Manager who is attending a company Board Meeting on the following day.

He is in a hurry to get off to meet his girlfriend after work and fails to check the figures he has input, some of which he has accidentally picked up from the previous financial year. He assumes they will be correct and says to a colleague 'this data should be okay because the spreadsheet is always accurate in its calculations'.

Verdict: the Finance Assistant is not taking due care in his professional duties. He has made mistakes which could create trouble for the Manager.

confidentiality

The Code defines confidentiality as:

The principle of confidentiality imposes an obligation on members to refrain from:

– disclosing outside the firm or employing organisation confidential information acquired as a result of professional and business relationships without proper and specific authority or unless there is a legal or professional right or duty to disclose; and

– using confidential information acquired as a result of professional and business relationships to their personal advantage or the advantage of third parties

Confidentiality is the duty not to disclose information held by the business about another person or organisation to anyone else, unless permission has been given by that person or organisation.

The type of information that should not be given to outsiders includes personal or business details of:

▩ customers and clients

▩ suppliers

▩ colleagues

▩ internal information about the organisation

'Outsiders' who should not be given information include:

▩ family members

▩ social acquaintances

▩ 'cold callers', eg marketing survey companies

Here are some examples of incorrect behaviour by employees in the finance function:

breaches of confidentiality

1 A customer telephones and asks a newly-appointed accounts assistant what rate of trade discount another customer receives. The accounts assistant looks it up and tells the customer on the phone that it is 35%.

Verdict: the accounts assistant has breached confidentiality in giving out details of another customer.

2 A man contacts a business and speaks to a finance assistant. The man wants the mobile number of the finance assistant's colleague. He says that the matter is urgent and he is a good friend of the colleague. The finance assistant looks on his mobile and gives him the number.

Verdict: the accounts assistant has breached confidentiality in giving out details of a colleague.

3 An accounts receivable assistant asks a payroll assistant (a good friend) what the salary of the accounts receivable line manager is, as she too wants to become a line manager. The payroll assistant agrees to look it up in the payroll system and gives her the information.

Verdict: the payroll assistant has breached confidentiality in giving out internal confidential information.

confidentiality – the Data Protection Act

As we have seen in Chapter 5, The **Data Protection Act 2018** is the UK law which protects **personal data** from being released to outsiders and makes it an offence to release this information without permission from the person whose data it is. The Act covers:

- data about individuals (eg sole traders) but **not** about limited companies

- records held on computer – eg a computer database of names, addresses, telephone numbers, sales details of each customer

- manual records – ie paper documents, eg statements, letters

The Act states that the data held must be accurate, kept securely and made available on request to the person whose data is held on file.

situations where information can be disclosed

If there were no exceptions to the confidentiality rule, the transfer of information could become a problem, so the person or organisation whose information is involved can give **consent** for the release of the information. Accountants in practice, for example, will obtain permission from clients to release financial information to third parties.

Also note that:

- there is a **legal duty** to disclose information, eg if an employee suspects a client is involved in money laundering, ie transferring money received from criminal activity into an apparently legitimate account and so changing 'bad' money into 'good' money

- in some cases the disclosure is in the **public interest**, eg a client who appears to be involved in or funding terrorist activities

Here are some examples of these types of situation:

deciding if personal information can be disclosed

1 An accountancy firm doing an audit notices that the client is regularly receiving large sums of money from undocumented sources and is then transferring them into an overseas savings account.

   Verdict: the client appears to be laundering the funds and so the accountancy firm will need to disclose this information to the authorities.

2 Sid is a sole trader attempting to set up a credit card account in his name, but the request is refused. Sid asks the credit card company if he can see if there is anything in his credit history which is blocking the application.

   Verdict: the Data Protection Act 2018 states that he is entitled to see his credit history.

professional behaviour

The Code defines professional behaviour as:

The principle of professional behaviour imposes an obligation on members to comply with relevant laws and regulations and avoid any action that may bring disrepute to the profession. This includes actions which a reasonable and informed third party, having knowledge of all relevant information, would conclude negatively affect the good reputation of the profession.

Professional behaviour means not bringing the profession into disrepute by acting in ways that are unprofessional or not complying with laws and regulations.

COMPLYING WITH ETHICS

AAT Code of Professional Ethics

The AAT Code of Professional Ethics requires members to have a professional and ethical approach throughout their lives.

The Code covers the five fundamental ethical principles which members must follow, whilst protecting public interest and maintaining the good reputation of AAT.

The Code is based on the laws effective in the UK, which as a minimum, members are expected to comply with.

The Code states that members have a responsibility to act in the public interest. This means that members duties are not exclusively to satisfy the needs of an individual client or employer, but to ensure that they act responsibly in matters of public interest.

The Code states that members should take a conceptual framework approach to ethics. This means that if faced with an ethical decision, members should base their decision around the five fundamental principles and use their professional judgement when considering their decision.

threats to compliance

The Code states that when a member identifies threats to compliance with the fundamental principles, the member needs to determine whether appropriate safeguards are available and can be applied to eliminate the threats, or reduce them to an acceptable level.

Threats fall into the following categories:

■ self-interest threats, which may occur where a financial or other interest will inappropriately influence the member's judgment or behaviour

- self-review threats, which may occur when a previous judgement needs to be re-evaluated by the member responsible for that judgement

- advocacy threats, which may occur when a member promotes a position or opinion to the point that subsequent objectivity may be compromised

- familiarity threats, which may occur when a member becomes too sympathetic to the interests of others because of a close or personal relationship

- intimidation threats, which may occur when a member may be deterred from acting objectively by threats, whether actual or perceived

Safeguards are actions or other measures that may eliminate threats or reduce them to an acceptable level.

These fall into two broad categories:

- safeguards created by the profession, legislation or regulation, for example:

    - educational, training and experience requirements for entry into the profession

    - continuing professional development requirements

    - corporate governance regulations

    - professional standards

    - professional or regulatory monitoring and disciplinary procedures

    - external review of the reports, returns, communications or information produced by a member and carried out by a legally empowered third party

- safeguards in the work environment

If members are in doubt about the course of action that should be taken, they should contact the Ethics Advice Line at AAT for assistance.

breaches of the Code

Misconduct is professional or personal conduct that is in breach of the Code and poses a risk to the public or is likely to undermine the public confidence in AAT or its members.

Any complaint of misconduct is dealt with under disciplinary regulations by an investigations team and the member may have to face a disciplinary tribunal.

The sanctions which are available to the disciplinary tribunal include:

- the member could be expelled
- the member could be suspended
- specific conditions could be imposed on the member
- the member could receive a reprimand or warning
- the member could receive a fine
- a student member could have their registration withdrawn

The need to act ethically does not just apply to the accountancy profession. The organisations that employees work for will often also have ethical guides that employees must follow.

SUSTAINABILITY

sustainability – the three pillars

'**Sustainability**' is a term that describes the need for organisations and individuals to become 'green' and adopt policies which protect the environment, save energy and benefit society as a whole.

The three main objectives of sustainability, known as the 'three pillars of sustainability', are:

- economic growth
- environmental protection
- social equality

These are sometimes also referred to as the **triple bottom line**, 'profit, planet and people' – which is a useful way of remembering the three main objectives.

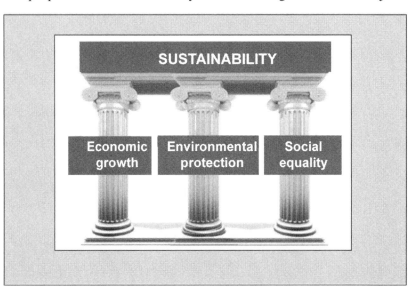

economic growth

Economic growth is important because it makes sustainable development possible. The term 'economic growth' relates to the making of profit by organisations that will bring financial benefits to owners, employees and to the economy locally and nationally.

Examples of the benefits of economic growth include:

- using company profits to make donations to national charities
- using company profits to support events in the local community

environmental protection

The need to protect the environment and conserve resources – the 'green' factor – is one that is most commonly associated with sustainability. Examples of 'green' policies which can be adopted by organisations include:

- initiatives in the workplace to reduce the consumption of electricity, eg 'turn off the lights and the computers at night' campaigns
- energy-saving devices such as LED and low-energy lights
- the use of recycled materials in the office, eg paper and printer toner cartridges
- using materials from sustainable resources (eg books, such as this one, printed on paper manufactured from forests which are being replanted rather than being depleted)
- recycling of waste materials, eg paper, plastic, cardboard
- reducing the 'carbon footprint', eg reducing CO_2 by introducing
  - cycle to work schemes
  - low-emission company cars
  - car sharing schemes
- requiring suppliers to certify their 'green' credentials, eg farmers supplying supermarkets being required to avoid the use of harmful pesticides

the financial implications of sustainability

The financial implications of sustainability can work in opposite ways on an organisation such as a large business:

- a sustainability policy can make the business **save money**, but also
- a sustainability policy can make the business incur **greater costs**

One of the major advantages of cutting down on the use of resources such as energy and paper is that it can **save money**. This means that it can actually pay a business to introduce 'green' policies, for example:

- a business that runs a fleet of fuel-efficient company cars will have lower fuel costs and receive tax benefits for using low emission vehicles

- the Government scheme whereby large retailers have to charge customers for plastic bags and give the money received to charitable causes has reduced the number of bags given out and the amount retailers spend on new bags – a saving which also benefits society

Both of these measures benefit the environment and society and cut the running costs of a business.

One of the issues of sustainability is that it sometimes requires businesses **to incur extra costs**, for example:

- ordering packaging made from recycled cardboard and plastics which are more expensive but have been specified by the business to prove its own 'green' credentials

- recycling the packaging used on deliveries from suppliers

- complying with regulations which require modifications to products to ensure that they are environmentally friendly – cars, for example

sustainability and social equality

Another important objective of sustainability is the social well-being of people, not just in one locality, but worldwide.

how can sustainability help?

As far as sustainability is concerned, 'society' includes a wide range of people and promoting 'social equality' involves many different ways of helping these people. A finance function of a business may get involved in all these areas:

- the **worldwide and national communities**

  - sponsoring events (eg sponsored walks and marathons) to raise funds for charitable causes, eg London Marathon, Comic Relief, Cancer Research UK

  - sponsoring sport and the arts

- the **local community**

  - sponsoring local sports events

  - providing work experience to local school students

  - providing prizes for school and college award ceremonies

- the **organisation** which employs finance staff

  - providing the funds and time off for an employee to take an accounting qualification

  - setting up and funding 'bonding' activities within the department, eg a night out, a white water rafting experience

a high quality product

Another benefit which an organisation can provide for its customers is a high quality of product or service. A product which is environmentally friendly and socially beneficial will help to increase sales and profitability.

CORPORATE SOCIAL RESPONSIBILITY (CSR)

promoting sustainable principles

Businesses such as limited companies and other organisations known to the general public like to promote themselves to their stakeholders and the public in general as being 'green' and socially responsible. This adoption of policies which promote the principles of sustainability is known as **corporate social responsibility**. By 'stakeholders' we mean all the people who have an interest in the business or organisation, for example:

- shareholders who have invested in them if they are public limited companies

- customers who buy from them

- suppliers who supply them

- the local community

- their employees

- the general public

sustainability and corporate social responsibility

The way in which organisations promote a 'green' and socially responsible image is by general advertising and also, in the case of the larger companies, by the issue of a **corporate social responsibility (CSR)** document, which is usually included within the financial statements.

Corporate social responsibility (CSR) initiatives include policies which

- help to protect the environment

- help society both locally and worldwide

- improve the welfare of the workforce

Examples of these are set out below.

protecting the environment

- installing low consumption electrical devices
- encouraging staff to save energy by checking that electrical equipment is turned off at the end of the working day
- reducing CO_2 (carbon dioxide) emissions from premises
- encouraging staff to use public transport rather than their own cars
- introducing 'cycle to work' and car sharing schemes
- recycling of waste material (eg paper, plastic and cardboard)

helping society locally and worldwide

- sourcing products where possible from renewable resources and where local economies will benefit (eg 'Fair Trade' coffee and bananas)
- ensuring that the supply chain (eg farmers who supply supermarkets) is also actively supporting sustainable development (environmentally and socially)
- sponsoring national fund raising events such as the London Marathon
- sponsoring local sports and arts events
- setting up links with local schools and colleges

improving the welfare of the workforce

- providing staff training and promotion prospects
- providing flexible working so that employees can meet personal commitments (eg picking up children from school)
- offering free gym membership to staff
- organising social events and 'bonding' events such as activity days out
- encouraging CPD (Continuing Professional Development), for example providing resources in terms of time and textbooks for professional courses

Organisations regularly review their CSR policies and commitments over time as their own goals and society evolve.

Chapter Summary

- Ethical behaviour in the workplace involves knowing about and practising basic principles of good and acceptable behaviour.

- Ethical behaviour in the workplace is based on a number of principles:

    - integrity

    - objectivity

    - professional competence and due care

    - confidentiality

    - professional behaviour

- These ethical principles should be observed not only in the workplace, but also out of working hours in situations such as social gatherings.

- The five ethical principles are referred to as the fundamental ethical principles in AAT's Code of Professional Ethics.

- **Sustainability** is a concept which drives the policies of most organisations.

- The three main objectives of sustainability – also known as the 'three pillars of sustainability' – are:

    - **economic growth**, ie creating profit for the benefit of business owners, employees and the economy in general

    - **environmental protection** – the 'green' factor

    - **social equality** – increasing the well-being of society at large

- Many organisations adopt the policies of sustainability through setting up various initiatives; these are collectively known as 'corporate social responsibility' and contain schemes for:

    - environmental protection

    - helping society locally and worldwide

    - improving the welfare of the workforce

workplace ethics	moral principles and standards which set out how employees should behave when they are at work and representing their employer away from the workplace
integrity	to be straightforward and honest in all professional and business relationships
objectivity	not to allow bias, conflict of interest or undue influence of others to override professional or business judgements
professional competence and due care	to maintain professional knowledge and skills at the required level
confidentiality	knowing when to disclose information held by the organisation and when not to disclose it
professional behaviour	to comply with relevant laws and regulations and not bringing the profession into disrepute
sustainability	policies adopted by people and organisations which are based on the principles of economic growth (profit), environmental protection (planet) and social equality (people)
economic growth	the ways in which the making of profit by a business benefits the business owners, employees and in varying degrees also benefits the local and national economies
environmental protection	policies adopted by organisations which protect and conserve natural resources
social equality	policies adopted by organisations which promote the well-being of people both locally and worldwide
corporate social responsibility	the overall strategy of an organisation promoting all areas of sustainability

Activities

8.1 You work in the Accounts Office of a large wholesaler.

Indicate which **one** of the following situations represents a breach of confidentiality.

(a)	You have been asked to send some figures to your company's auditors	
(b)	You email your company's Sales Manager with details of customer credit limits	
(c)	You mention to a member of your family that a shop in the High Street that is one of your customers is having financial problems and is likely to become insolvent	
(d)	One of your customers sends a letter asking you to send sales figures to the bank	

8.2 The three sentences in the table below represent breaches of ethical behaviour.

You are to write in the right-hand column the appropriate ethical principle which is breached in each case. Choose from:

integrity	**professional behaviour**	**confidentiality**
professional competence and due care		**objectivity**

You mention to your partner that her employer has been refused credit by the company that employs you.	
You 'borrow' £10 from the cash till because you are short of cash for the weekend. You fully intend to put it back on Monday, but you forget as it is such a busy day.	
You hear a colleague at a Friday night pub session in a crowded bar say that his manager is 'useless' and he 'doesn't know how he got his qualifications'.	

8.3 Indicate in the table below which **four** of the following are sustainability policies that a business might adopt.

(a)	A cycle to work scheme	
(b)	A policy of re-using the blank side of A4 white copy paper for printing on	
(c)	Testing the fire extinguishers on a regular basis	
(d)	Putting up a notice telling staff to only fill the kettle with the amount of water needed when making coffee or tea	
(e)	Using company cars which have the most powerful engines	
(f)	Suggesting a team is set up to do a charity walk in support of Cancer Research UK	
(g)	Making sure that everyone has a regular eye test	
(h)	Recommending that the cheapest packaging material is used to save money	

8.4 Indicate which **two** of the following statements is true in relation to sustainability.

(a)	Sustainability involves keeping sales of products at a stable level	
(b)	Computers should be turned off at the end of each working day	
(c)	Sustainability encourages an employer to pay for an employee to train for an accounting qualification	
(d)	It is best to keep lights on at all times because this will mean that the bulbs will last longer	

8.5 You work for a restaurant chain 'Pronta Pizza' as a Management Trainee. Your team has been asked by the Training Manager to investigate various initiatives that could be incorporated into a corporate social responsibility plan for next year. The initiatives must relate to the three principles of sustainability:

- Protecting the environment
- Providing a benefit to the Pronta Pizza employees
- Helping society locally and nationally

The list of initiatives which the team then suggests is shown below:

Suggested initiatives for the corporate social responsibility plan

(1) Save electricity and gas by not having the ovens on continuously

(2) Divide all tips received between all the employees and ensure that they are not taken by the management

(3) Pay for staff to go on a part-time catering course

(4) Ensure that tips only go to the waiting staff because the kitchen staff do not meet the public

(5) Have 'Please recycle me!' printed on takeaway pizza boxes

(6) Re-use paper napkins which appear to be clean to save on paper wastage

(7) Buy fresh salad and vegetables from local organic suppliers

(8) Display collection boxes for Oxfam in the restaurants

(9) Charge customers £1 extra for take-away pizza boxes

(10) Publicise a 'two for one pizza' special offer for students and senior citizens

---

Tasks

(a) The Training Manager reads through the list and asks you to identify and comment on three suggestions which you think would not work as initiatives because they do not comply with the principles of sustainability or with workplace regulations. Set them out in the table below.

(b) You are then asked to sort the remaining listed suggestions into the three sustainability categories and enter them in the table below:

Protecting the environment
Providing a benefit to the Pronta Pizza employees
Helping society locally and nationally

(c) If, as suggested in this scenario, the restaurant management might be taking the tips given to the waiting staff, this would be which of the following (tick the correct answer).

(a)	Contrary to the sustainability principle which protects the environment	
(b)	A breach of the ethical requirement of integrity	
(c)	A breach of the ethical requirement of confidentiality	
(d)	Acceptable practice	

Answers to chapter activities

CHAPTER 1: AN INTRODUCTION TO BUSINESS

1.1 **(a)** Further education colleges = not-for-profit

(b) Chain of pubs = profit

(c) Children's hospice = not-for-profit

(d) Online bookshop = profit

1.2 (c) to maximise profit

1.3 False

1.4 (c) a private limited company

1.5 (d) £50,000

1.6 **(a)** Company = dividends

(b) Partnership = drawings

(c) Sole trader = drawings

1.7 Two advantages and two disadvantages of a business operating as a partnership.

advantages (any two):	disadvantages (any two):
growth potential	no overall control
shared skills and knowledge	shared profits
shared responsibility	shared liability of debts
simple to set up	disputes between partners

1.8 The sources of finance will depend on the cost of the equipment and the size of the business; however, a sole trader business will be relatively small. The funds available include:

- further capital from the owner
- bank loans
- loans from other individuals
- bank overdrafts
- credit cards
- credit from suppliers
- leasing the equipment

1.9 Contents of the financial statements of a large public limited company:

- statement of profit or loss
- statement of financial position
- notes to the financial statements
- statement of cashflows
- statement of changes in equity
- directors report
- auditors report

1.10 (a) income tax

(c) national insurance

(d) VAT

1.11 The activities relate to:

Business activity	Business function
Monitoring the training needs of employees	Human resources
Negotiating with suppliers the quantities of material required for production	Operations
Dealing with the transport of products overseas	Distribution and logistics

CHAPTER 2: THE EXTERNAL BUSINESS ENVIRONMENT

2.1   (c)   the exchange rate

2.2   (a)   jewellery shop

(d)   travel agent

2.3   (b)   rise

2.4   (c)   someone without a job who is actively seeking employment

2.5   (a)   EU goods would become cheaper to buy in the UK

2.6   (a)   savings

2.7   **False**   A business which has offices in several countries must perform all financial operations in one country.
True   A business which operates globally has an increased risk of its data being compromised.

2.8   As prices increase, demand will **fall** and supply will **rise.**

2.9   **Risk**   - something negative may happen in the future, but it can be measured with some probability.
Uncertainty   - happens due to events outside of the control of a business and the outcome is unknown, it cannot be measured.

2.10   Four ways a government attempts to control an economy:

- growth
- inflation
- employment
- balance of payments

2.11   Three examples of direct tax:

- income tax
- corporation tax
- inheritance tax

2.12   Four stages of the economic cycle:

- boom
- slowdown
- recession
- recovery

CHAPTER 3: RULES AND REGULATIONS FOR BUSINESS

3.1   (c)   the Lord Chief Justice

3.2   (b)   Jury

3.3   (c)   Damages

3.4   **(a)**   Theft = criminal law

    (b)   Breach of contract = civil law

    (c)   Negligence = civil law

    (d)   Terrorism = criminal law

3.5   (b)   administrative law

    (d)   human rights law

3.6   (b)   The promise by both parties to exchange value

3.7   (d)   The checkout assistant scans the milk and the price shows on the display

3.8   **False**   The agreement was not set up with the intention to create legal relations

3.9   (b)   An invitation to treat

3.10   (b)   A voidable contract

3.11   **(a)**   false

    (b)   false

3.12   To register as a sole trader:

- national insurance number
- contact details
- date of registration
- if previously registered, the unique tax reference

3.13   To register as a private limited company with Companies House:

- name and address
- details of directors and shareholders
- share capital details
- memorandum and articles of association

CHAPTER 4: THE FINANCE FUNCTION

4.1   (d)   It deals with cash, financial records, financial reports, costing and budgets

4.2   (a)   HM Revenue & Customs

       (c)   The company's bank

       (d)   The customers of the business

       (f)   The suppliers of the business

4.3   (a)   Prepares the financial statements of a business

4.4   An **internal auditor** is normally an employee of the organisation being audited, but an **external auditor** should be a member of an independent firm of accountants.

4.5   (a)   Being successful in achieving what you set out to do

4.6   (b)   To complete a job with the minimum of wasted time, effort or expense

4.7   (b)   It must be made within an appropriate timescale

       (c)   It needs to be made using language appropriate to the situation

4.8   (a)   Details of the authorisation needed for business purchases

4.9   (c)   Being able to pay all company debts when they are due

4.10 (b)   Get customers to pay earlier

4.11 (a)   • receivables ledger assistant to accounts line manager

            • cashier to accounts line manager

            • payroll assistant to accounts line manager

       (b)   the receivables ledger assistant

       (c)   examples include payables ledger, management accounting, inventory control

CHAPTER 5: FINANCIAL INFORMATION AND DATA SECURITY

5.1   A certificate of incorporation for a company and an Act of Parliament are primary sources.

A tutorial book about personal tax is a secondary source.

5.2   (c)   consistent information

5.3   (b)   The total may not agree with the total on the statement of account sent by the seller

5.4   (a)   The product code may not agree with the description of the goods and so it will need to be queried

5.5   (b)   The amounts sent by the buyer in settlement of invoices must be correctly shown on the statement

5.6   Favourable variance: sales are higher than budgeted, costs are lower than budgeted

Adverse variance: sales are lower than budgeted, costs are higher than budgeted

5.7   (c)   Preparing a cash budget

5.8   (b)   A statement of profit or loss

5.9   (c)   Not releasing personal data to outsiders

5.10   1   pass2A%

        2   G5Thrones

        3   kith33

        4   mypassword

5.11   (a)   At least daily

        (b)   In more than one storage format

        (e)   Stored on the premises and also externally

CHAPTER 6: BUSINESS COMMUNICATIONS

6.1   (d)   The message must be clear, correct and on time

6.2   (b) and (c)

6.3   (d)

6.4   (b) and (c)

6.5   **(a)** They're, **(b)** their, **(c)** There

6.6

Title page
(Executive) Summary
Introduction
Findings (Main Body)
Conclusions
Recommendations
Appendices

6.7

Incorrect word	Correction
239847244	239847224
Mrs	Miss
Colman	Coleman
dissappointed	disappointed
They're	There
faithfully	sincerely

6.8   **(a)** and **(b)**

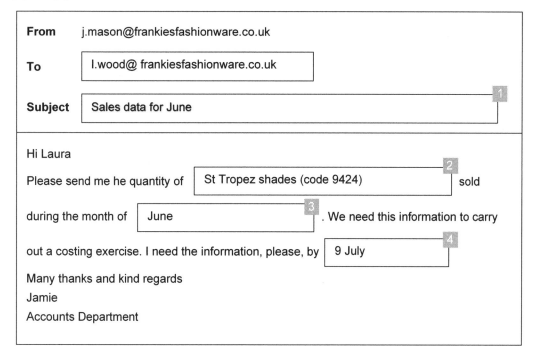

From	j.mason@frankiesfashionware.co.uk
To	l.wood@ frankiesfashionware.co.uk
Subject	Sales data for June 1

Hi Laura

Please send me he quantity of | St Tropez shades (code 9424)   2 | sold

during the month of | June   3 | . We need this information to carry

out a costing exercise. I need the information, please, by | 9 July   4 |

Many thanks and kind regards

Jamie

Accounts Department

6.9   **(a)**   Missing: name or signature of the person who has written the message, no indication of the percentage discount to be given.

   (b)   Missing: date, person or department to contact at RF Electronics

6.10   Possible situations might include:

- making an important telephone call which involves complex data
- preparing for a staff appraisal
- preparing a verbal presentation
- attending an important meeting at which you want to bring up a number of different issues
- a 'report back' to colleagues about an internal meeting you have attended
- a 'report back' to colleagues about a meeting with an important customer or supplier

CHAPTER 7: PLANNING AND MANAGING YOUR WORK

7.1 (c) Carry on with your own work until you have the opportunity to refer the problem to your line manager when she is free

7.2

Your line manager asks you for the balances of your top 20 customer accounts. She needs the information for a meeting that morning.	**urgent**
Your line manager asks you to provide information from the office for the accountants who are coming in next week to audit the accounts. You have never done this before as this is normally a senior colleague's responsibility	**one-off 'ad hoc'**
Your colleague reminds you that it is your turn to get the milk from Tesco Express and remarks that the milk has run out.	**non-urgent**

7.3

Category of task	Reason
urgent and important	if you don't do this task soon you are going to let a lot of people down
urgent but less important	your manager asks you to turn down the heating
important but not urgent	setting up a spreadsheet for a meeting in a week's time
neither important nor urgent	sending round a suggestion list for a staff social

7.4

An employee's personal record of tasks and events over a long period of time.	**diary**
A detailed plan which involves a number of people and interrelated tasks and events for a specific purpose over a period of time.	**action plan**
An annual guide which can be used to display staff holidays and external training courses.	**wall planner**
An employee's daily personal record of tasks to be done in the short term.	**'to do' list**

Task 7.5

(a)

WEDNESDAY/THURSDAY/FRIDAY 'TO DO' LIST (in order of completion)	
Task 1	Process the payroll (BACS and cash)
Task 2	Update and balance the petty cash book
Task 3	Visit the bank to pick up cash wages and petty cash top up
Task 4	Lock the cash in the safe at work
Task 5	Make up cash pay packets and distribute payslips for all employees

(b)

	Serious	Not serious
The staff may not get paid on time	✔	
The cash from the bank may not get locked away	✔	
Petty cash reimbursements may be delayed		✔
Suppliers may not get paid on time	✔	
Minor office duties may not get done		✔

CHAPTER 8: ETHICS, SUSTAINABILITY AND CORPORATE SOCIAL RESPONSIBILITY

8.1 (c) You mention to a member of your family that a shop in the High Street that is one of your customers is having financial problems and is likely to become insolvent

8.2

You mention to your partner that her employer has been refused credit by the company that employs you.	confidentiality
You 'borrow' £10 from the cash till because you are short of cash for the weekend. You fully intend to put it back on Monday, but you forget as it is such a busy day.	integrity
You hear a colleague at a Friday night pub session in a crowded bar say that his manager is 'useless' and he 'doesn't know how he got his qualifications'.	professional behaviour

8.3 (a) A cycle to work scheme

(b) A policy of re-using the blank side of A4 white copy paper for printing on

(d) Putting up a notice telling staff to only fill the kettle with the amount of water needed when making coffee or tea

(f) Suggesting a team is set up to do a charity walk in support of Cancer Research UK

8.4 (b) Computers should be turned off at the end of each working day

(c) Sustainability encourages an employer to pay for an employee to train for an accounting qualification

8.5 (a) (4) Ensure that tips only go to the waiting staff because the kitchen staff do not meet the public

(Comment: this would be very unfair on the kitchen staff)

(6) Re-use paper napkins which appear to be clean to save on paper wastage

(Comment: this would be very unhygienic and contrary to health and safety principles)

(9) Charge customers £1 extra for take-away pizza boxes

(Comment: this would be unpopular with customers as they are used to having free boxes. The suggestion for 'Please recycle me!' printed on the box would be far more effective.)

(b)   **Protecting the environment**

    (1)   Save electricity and gas by not having the ovens on continuously

    (5)   Have 'Please recycle me!' printed on takeaway pizza boxes

    (7)   Buy fresh salad and vegetables from local organic suppliers

Providing a benefit to the Pronta Pizza employees

    (2)   Divide all tips received between all the employees and ensure that they are not taken by the management

    (3)   Pay for staff to go on a part-time catering course

Helping society locally and nationally

    (8)   Display collection boxes for Oxfam in the restaurants

    (10)   Publicise a 'two for one pizza' special offer for students and senior citizens

(c)   (b)   A breach of the ethical requirement of integrity

Index

for your notes

for your notes

for your notes

for your notes

_____

for your notes

for your notes

for your notes

for your notes

for your notes